a handful of herbs

a handful of herbs

Inspiring ideas for gardening, cooking and decorating your home with herbs

Barbara Segall • Louise Pickford • Rose Hammick

with photography by Caroline Arber and William Lingwood

RYLAND PETERS & SMALL

LONDON • NEW YORK

Designer Barbara Zuñiga
Picture Manager Christina Borsi
Editor Alice Sambrook
Production Controller Mai-Ling Collyer
Art Director Leslie Harrington
Editorial Director Julia Charles
Publisher Cindy Richards

Indexer Hilary Bird

First published in the United Kingdom in 2001
This revised and updated edition published in 2016
by Ryland Peters & Small
20–21 Jockey's Fields
London WC1R 4BW
and
341 East 116th Street
New York NY 10029

www.rylandpeters.com

10 9 8 7 6 5 4 3 2 1

ISBN 978-1-84975-719-5

Printed and bound in China

A CIP record for this book is available from the British Library.
CIP data from the Library of Congress has been applied for.

The information contained herein is not intended to be
a substitute for professional medical advice or treatment.
Essential oils should not be used undiluted nor taken
internally except on medical advice. No responsibility
for any problem arising from their use is accepted by
the authors or publisher.

contents

introduction

Every one of us feels that our own garden is a particular paradise, but the herb garden has the edge on them all. There is nothing quite like the rush of sensual pleasure that comes from simply brushing against a lavender bush, or stepping across a thyme or chamomile path.

These attractions don't end in the garden. Herbs can be brought into the house to be used fresh in cooking, or dried, frozen or otherwise preserved for later use. Some can be transformed into potpourri or used in different ways to perfume and decorate rooms, or to freshen drawers and clothes, while others fragrance baths or become simple, gentle cosmetics and lotions.

Gardeners of the past discovered, probably through trial and error, which plants were safe to use in food and for healing. Down the centuries herbs and other useful plants have come into our lives courtesy of various waves of invaders, travellers and soldiers. Herbs were first appreciated for their medicinal qualities. In Western history, the medicinal use of herbs dates from the first century AD, when the Greek physician Dioscorides set out the healing properties of more than 500 plants in what was one of the first descriptive herbals, his *De Materia Medica*.

In the herb gardens of today it is not uncommon to find the culinary, medicinal and folkloric traditions of the past combined with a modern appreciation of attractive plant forms. Most herb gardens are now enjoyed for the power-packed aromatic leaves of herbs such as rosemary, sage, thyme, lovage and chives, as well as for the simple but enchanting flowers and useful seeds that many herbs offer. It is this continuity of the past in our present homes that makes the bountiful summer harvest of these useful plants so evocative and especially satisfying.

If asked to define a herb, most people would say it is a plant used in cooking, but the true definition of the term is much wider. It includes trees, shrubs, biennials, annuals and herbaceous perennials that have culinary, aromatic, medicinal and cosmetic uses. In addition, many are excellent decorative garden plants. Some herbs are used for their foliage and flowers, others for their seeds or roots, and some for all four attributes.

Barbara Segall

LEFT **Basil's aromatic leaves and flowers add interest to many dishes and desserts.**

super herbs

With an ancient record in folklore and medicinal history, basil is also a highly distinctive culinary herb, especially in Asian, French and Italian cuisines.

basil
Ocimum basilicum

Best used freshly picked, basil can also be frozen in leaf form or in made-up sauces. It combines well with tomatoes for a salad and is the main ingredient of pesto sauce for pasta. It adds piquancy to pizzas and to chicken and lamb dishes.

There are at least 13 different types of basil, varying in foliage, colour, shape, texture and aroma. Flavours range from aniseed to cinnamon and the sweet, spicy, clove-like scent of sweet basil. Basil can grow up to 45 cm (18 in).

O. basilicum 'Purpurascens' has purple leaves and pinkish flowers. *O. basilicum* 'Citriodorum' is lemon-scented with green leaves and white flowers. Anise-flavoured basil has pale pink flowers and a strong taste of aniseed. The tiny leaves of Greek basil, which grows in the shape of a small bush, offer the fullest flavour.

Plant basil in a herb garden or in containers in late summer, when there is no danger of frost or severely cold weather. In the herb garden grow it in a sheltered sunny site in light well-drained soil. If grown on in a container, basil should be kept well watered in dry conditions.

Basil has traditional uses as a digestive aid and a herbal tonic, as well as being used in aromatherapy.

bay
Laurus nobilis

Glossy dark-green bay
leaves are part
of the bouquet garni, the traditional herb
bundle used to add flavour to savoury dishes.
Bay is also a good flavouring for sweet dishes,
particularly rice puddings and other milk desserts;
its delicate spiciness can be best enjoyed if the
milk is simmered gently with the bay leaf before
the other ingredients are added.

An evergreen tree with shiny aromatic,
spicy leaves, small yellow flowers and
black berries, bay can grow to 8 m (26 ft) but is
generally slow-growing, and in containers its height is
controlled. It can be clipped into geometric shapes or
grown as an elegant ornamental standard.
Shaped bay trees in pots are also useful in
herb gardens as focal points to mark the
meeting of paths or to emphasize a change of height.

Buy young plants and plant them in spring or
autumn in rich, well-drained soil. Although bay will
tolerate light shade, it prefers full sun. Protect young
plants and plants in containers from frost with straw
bales, bubble wrap or hessian windbreaks. Cut back
any frost-damaged stems in spring. Pick leaves as
needed throughout the year.

L. nobilis 'Aurea' has golden leaves and makes
an attractive colour contrast in the herb garden.
L. nobilis 'Angustifolia', the willowleaf bay, is also
attractive as a container plant and in the garden.

Infusions made from bay leaves have been used
to stimulate appetite or as an aid to digestion.

**Bay leaves were the foliage
used in wreaths to garland
winners and achievers in
classical Greece and Rome.**

A pineapple-like scent floats in the air when the leaves are crushed underfoot or gently squeezed between the fingers.

chamomile
Chamaemelum nobile

This hardy evergreen perennial is distinguished by flowers that resemble daisies, finely cut foliage – and a perfume that takes your breath away. Chamomile is widely used in cosmetics, soothing skin creams and other medications. Its dried flowers can be steeped in hot water to make a relaxing tisane, but it has no culinary uses. The creeping, non-flowering variety of chamomile tolerates light traffic, making it suitable for covering a short length of path or the ground under a bench.

Grow chamomile in light well-drained soil in full sun. It can reach 20 cm (8 in) in height. Chamomile paths should be kept weed-free or the weeds will overwhelm the chamomile plants, eventually destroying the fragrant pathway.

Non-flowering lawn chamomile, C. nobile 'Treneague', which has fern-like leaves, is used to create scented lawns and paths. Upright chamomile, which has daisy-like blooms, is grown in the border for its flowers, which can be used fresh or dried. The double-flowered form, C. nobile 'Flore Pleno', is an attractive addition to the garden, and its flowers are used to make chamomile tea.

The flowers, single or double, of upright chamomile have medicinal and cosmetic uses in facial steam baths and hair rinses; they also bring a soothing and relaxing fragrance to a bath. Dried flowers and leaves of chamomile can be added to potpourri.

chervil

Anthriscus cerefolium

A refreshing salad herb, chervil is also useful as a feathery and flavoursome garnish. Its light taste combines well with eggs, poultry and soft cheese. Although best used fresh, the leaves can be preserved by being frozen in ice-cube containers.

Chervil is a hardy annual with pretty fern-like leaves and small delicate white flowers in late summer. It grows up to 60 cm (23 in), thriving in a shady site in light well-drained soil. If planted as an inter-row crop, chervil takes advantage of shade from other row-crop plants. It dislikes root disturbance, so sow it direct into the growing site. Water plants well or they will bolt, flowering and setting seed too quickly, and you will lose flavoursome foliage. Pick the leaves through the summer.

Chervil plants can be grown indoors on a shady north-facing windowsill, but indoor plants will lack the vigour and flavour of plants grown outdoors. You can also sow seed in late summer for a winter crop, which will need some protection through the winter.

Rich in vitamins, chervil has traditionally been used as a treatment for digestive and circulatory disorders.

Chervil is highly prized in France, where it is often used in omelettes and as a component of the traditional *fines herbes* mixture.

Chives (left) bring a hint of onion to garnishes and salads, while coriander/cilantro (right) adds piquancy to curries and other hot dishes.

chives and garlic chives
Allium schoenoprasum and *A. tuberosum*

Chives have spiky green leaves and mauve flowers, while garlic chives, or Chinese chives, have garlic flavour in their strappy leaves and white starry flowers that appear in late summer. The chopped leaves of both types combine well with egg dishes and are useful for garnishes and in salads. Chives are also among the ingredients of the *fines herbes* mixture.

With their attractive flowers and good foliage, chives fit well into the flower garden. They make an informal edging for part of a kitchen garden and, if planted into spaces in paving, will eventually spread to make their own shapely patterns in the paving gaps.

The spiky leaves shoot from the underground mini-bulbs in spring. They grow to about 30 cm (12 in) but can be harvested once they are about 10 cm (4 in) above ground. Either pull leaves from the clump or cut off a handful with a pair of sharp scissors.

In late spring even spikier shoots carrying the flower buds start to appear. Chive flowers come in a range of pinky-mauve tones, as well as in a new form that is green to white. The flower heads, made up of numerous tiny flowers, are also edible and look attractive in salads. They are at their juicy best just as the buds begin to open.

Chives grow well in containers but will need extra attention to prevent them from drying out. Young plants can be kept on a windowsill or planted out in the sunniest site in the garden.

coriander
Coriandrum sativum

A strongly aromatic, short-lived annual, coriander/cilantro is grown for its seeds and for its deeply cut, parsley-like leaves that bring spice and flavour to desserts and savoury dishes alike. It bears a profusion of tiny white flowers. For the full effect of their flavour to be appreciated, coriander/cilantro leaves should be added towards the end of the cooking time.

The pinkish-white flowers that appear from early summer are followed by bead-like seeds, which are used in baking cakes and biscuits as well as in curries, chutneys and pickles. The leaves are added to stews and salads or used as a garnish. Plants grow to a height of about 60 cm (24 in).

In seed catalogues some varieties of coriander/cilantro may be described as 'slow to bolt', which means they will produce abundant well-flavoured foliage before they flower and set seed. To make sure you have a continuity of leaves, sow a little and often.

Coriander/cilantro grows well in a sunny spot in light well-drained soil. It needs a long hot summer for best seed production. Sow seeds in spring into the growing site and cover them with a cloche until established. Young plants should be kept well-watered and free of weeds. Pick young leaves before the mature ferny leaves develop.

Seeds tend to fall before they can be harvested, so the flower heads need to be picked before the seeds are fully ripe. Cover the flower heads and store them in a warm, dry, airy place so that the seeds can ripen. Collect and store the seeds in an airtight jar.

dill

Anethum graveolens

An excellent partner for fish in any form, hot or cold, dill is particularly renowned as an ingredient of the Scandinavian marinated-salmon dish gravadlax. Its fresh young leaves bring spice to salads, egg dishes and soups. The seeds, together with the flower heads, are used in pickles, preserves and chutneys. They are tasty with rice and cabbage, or as a flavouring for savoury bread, and are also used ground in curries.

A hardy annual with aromatic feathery leaves and clusters of yellow flowers in midsummer, dill grows to between 60 cm (2 ft) and 150 cm (5 ft), depending on variety. The seed needs well-drained soil, full sun and a sheltered site. Sow in the herb garden in spring, once the soil has warmed up. Since dill grows tall, it is not ideal in containers, but they can be useful for a first sowing.

Water seedlings and thin out to 20 cm (8 in). If necessary, support plants with a light framework of hazel twigs. Water regularly in dry seasons, or the plants will bolt and flower, and leaf harvest will be minimal. Pick leaves as needed when they are fresh and young.

Harvest seeds for culinary use before they ripen completely on the plant. Cut the flower heads off the plant, put them in paper bags and leave them to ripen in a warm dry place. When the seeds are dried, clean off the husks and store the seeds in airtight jars, ready for use.

Many seed companies differentiate between leaf and seed dill. *Anethum graveolens* 'Fernleaf' is a variety grown for high yields of leaves with short stems. *A. graveolens* 'Mammoth' is particularly good for seed production, while *A. graveolens* 'Dukat' is selected for its good leaf production. (All these varieties also produce good seeds.)

Dill is used as a calming treatment for upset stomachs and to alleviate insomnia. Ground seeds are sometimes used as a substitute for salt.

A cleansing spiciness is dill's gift to fish, soups and salads.

fennel
Foeniculum vulgare

This herb's bright-green leaf shoots unfurl in spring from pale leaf sheaths in which they are tightly packed like small parcels, scented with an unmistakable aroma. Fennel is distinct from Florence fennel, which is grown as a vegetable. The leaves are a flavoursome addition to salads and soups and make a good garnish. Bronze and green fennel can be combined to make a topping for salads. Both types are good partners for fish dishes. The seeds are also used in cooking and to make teas or tisanes. The flower heads can be used in pickling, and the leaves for flavouring oils and vinegars.

Fennel is a hardy perennial grown for its finely cut aromatic leaves in spring and summer and umbels of small yellow flowers in summer. It can grow to more than 2 m (6½ ft) and self-seeds – so be ruthless when you see fennel seedlings in spring. The ornamental quality of its foliage makes bronze fennel, *Foeniculum vulgare* 'Purpurascens', rewarding to grow. It has chocolate-brown feathery leaves, which contrast well with the green of ordinary fennel. The aroma is the same.

Grow fennel in a sunny site in rich well-drained soil. Sow into the growing site in late spring, or in containers in a greenhouse for earlier germination. Either thin or transplant, leaving a space of 50 cm (20 in) between plants.

Pick fennel leaves as needed through the spring and summer. The seeds should be harvested in autumn when they are ripe. Divide established plants of common fennel in spring or autumn. Try to segregate plantings of dill and fennel, or they will cross-pollinate.

Fennel has traditionally been used as a treatment for a wide range of conditions, but it is now most closely associated with the prevention of obesity.

Fennel's wispy foliage is one of the delights of the herb garden in spring.

Individual cloves of garlic can be used whole or chopped, crushed, or roasted in their skins to flavour savoury dishes, salads, salad dressings and bread.

garlic
Allium sativum

Several separate small cloves wrapped in a paper-thin skin that ranges in colour from rose-mauve to white are the components of a garlic bulb. Bulbs bought fresh from French markets or home-grown have an unbeatable flavour. Garlic is the main ingredient of many typical Mediterranean sauces, such as aioli, and is also valued for its health-giving effects.

Garlic has leek- or onion-like foliage and can grow up to 60 cm (24 in). It does best if grown in fertile well-drained soil in a sunny position. Plant individual cloves in spring, in rows 30 cm (12 in) apart, and keep them well watered, especially in dry periods.

Lift bulbs in summer and leave them on racks or in wooden boxes to dry off for a day or two in good weather; then hang them up in bunches in a dry, airy shed.

There are several different varieties of garlic available, with varying strengths of flavour; bulb and clove sizes also vary. *A. sativum* has white flowers, while *A. scorodoprasum* (also called rocambole) has a mild-flavoured bulb as well as edible bulbils mixed with flowers on its flower heads. Elephant garlic, *A. ampeloprasum* – which has a huge single onion-like bulb – is often available at supermarkets. Buy several bulbs, some to use and some to plant for next year's crop.

Traditionally used in the treatment of many conditions, garlic has been shown to lower blood pressure slightly and to boost the body's immunity to infections; it also has antiseptic qualities.

Long valued for its cleansing properties, and associated with fresh-smelling linen, lavender takes its name from the Latin for 'to wash'.

lavender
Lavandula species

Lavender flowers can be used in baking and jam-making or to flavour sugar. More often, the dried flowers and foliage are used to perfume rooms or packed into muslin/cheesecloth sachets and hung up in wardrobes. Flowers destined for potpourri or for making up into lavender bottles or bunches should be harvested as soon as they open, when the colour and aroma are at their most intense.

With grey-green, softly textured, highly aromatic leaves and (depending on species and variety) deep-blue, purple, white or pink flowers, this evergreen shrub grows up to 1 m (40 in). It thrives in a sunny, open site in well-drained, slightly sandy soil. *L. angustifolia* 'Hidcote', which has a uniform, compact shape and produces very deep-blue flowers, is a good choice for edging a path or small border. There are also forms with green, white or red flowers. Some lavenders, including *L. stoechas* and woolly lavender, *L. lanata*, are less hardy and need winter protection.

Lavender is useful as an edging or a hedging plant for a path or small parterre. Provided that you use plants of the same species or variety, the uniformity of shape and colour make it useful in formal as well as informal situations. It tolerates clipping into a variety of shapes. Cut back any woody stems in autumn and remove spent flower heads left on the plant from the previous season's flowering. Sow fresh seed in late summer or autumn. Transplant seedlings to 60 cm (24 in) apart or 30 cm (12 in) if growing as a hedge. Take cuttings in summer.

Lavender has been used therapeutically for its calming effects, as well as in the production of cosmetics and perfumes.

lemon balm

Melissa officinalis

A powerful lemon scent, released when its leaves are brushed against, and a fresh zesty flavour help to tip the balance in favour of lemon balm, which can become invasive in a small garden. It grows in soft mounded shapes that suit the front of a border. Leaves of lemon balm give a strong citrus flavour to salads.

Lemon balm is a hardy perennial, growing to 1 m (40 in) when in flower. Its rather insignificant flowers are carried on untidy-looking stems from the height of summer to autumn. Lemon balm can be useful for areas in shade, as long as it is planted in well-drained but moist soil.

The *Melissa officinalis* plant has plain green leaves. *M. officinalis* 'Aurea' is a golden-and-green variegated form that is very useful for introducing bold splashes of colour to the herb garden. *M. officinalis* 'All Gold' has yellow foliage.

The variegated form of lemon balm in particular combines well with other plants, but its flower stems should be snipped off to encourage leaf production. Once the flowers have formed, the yellow variegation tends to deteriorate.

Cut back flowering stems in late autumn to contain the tendency to self-seed. Pick leaves when required for fresh use and to dry or freeze. Sow seed in spring and divide established plants in autumn or spring.

A few leaves of fresh lemon balm in boiled water make a tasty tea, which has traditionally been used to relieve the symptoms of stress and tension.

To make the most effective herbal tea, harvest lemon balm before it comes into flower, when the essential oils are at their strongest.

lovage
Levisticum officinale

Lovage has a strong spicy flavour and a long history in traditional English cookery. Its foliage slightly resembles that of celery.

A hardy perennial with large dark-green leaves, lovage can grow up to a height of 2 m (6½ ft). Clusters of small pale-ochre flowers, resembling those of parsley, appear in late summer. It does best in a sunny site in rich well-drained soil. Plants should be watered regularly until established.

Lovage looks attractive near angelica, and if grown at the base of a rose will hide the rose's bare stems. Divide plants in spring or autumn every two or three years. Pick leaves when they are needed and seeds when they are ripe.

Lovage adds spiciness to food. Fresh leaves and stalks can be sprinkled into soups and stews for a meaty flavour, or blanched and eaten as a vegetable. Young leaves are delicious in salads and make an elegant garnish for savoury dishes. Seeds are sometimes added to biscuits before baking. They can be crushed and used as an ingredient of mixed-herb marinades, and are valued as a remedy for digestive complaints.

Lovage has a height and stature that make it useful as a tall accent plant at the centre of a kitchen herb garden.

mint

Mentha species

Chop mint into vinegar and mix it with sugar and a little warm water to make mint sauce, the natural accompaniment for roast lamb. Mint jelly, made with apples and mint, is also satisfying with lamb dishes. In Middle Eastern countries mint is used in cooked and cold food, as well as in drinks such as mint tea.

The genus *Mentha* includes some 25 species of perennials grown for their leaves, which are usually oval to lance-shaped and toothed at the edges. The ornamental flowers, ranging from deep mauve to light pinky-lavender in colour, attract bees and butterflies.

Mint thrives in full sun in well-drained but moist soil. Set young plants out in spring or autumn, and divide clumps that are growing in the ground in autumn. Mint will grow equally well in light shade and, as long as there is a source of water, provides good ground cover. To restrict its rapid sprawling growth, plant mint in a deep plastic or tin container, and sink the container into the ground.

Gingermint (*Mentha* x *gracilis* 'Variegata') has a spicy flavour and green leaves splashed with yellow. Pineapple mint (*M. suaveolens* 'Variegata') has woolly-textured green leaves, marked irregularly with creamy white, usually at the margins. Spearmint (*M. spicata*) and peppermint (*M.* x *piperita*) – both vigorous, spreading plants with attractive flowers – have the flavour traditionally associated with mint. Probably the most highly scented variety is lemon or eau-de-Cologne mint (*M.* x *piperita* 'Citrata'), which has a bronze tone to its leaves and stems. The perfume of its leaves is overwhelming if it is eaten, so it is better enjoyed as an aromatic foliage plant.

Mint is at its most aromatic before it comes into flower, so cut it back to encourage leaf production. Harvest the leaves through the growing season – they can be used fresh or dried, or frozen for later use. Mint may succumb to mint rust, which shows as rusty markings on the leaves. Remove affected plants and burn them, sterilize the soil, and replant with new healthy plants in another part of the garden.

Every herb garden should have at least one type of mint. With aromas and flavours for all occasions, mints also have much to offer in the shape of ornamental leaves and flowers.

oregano or marjoram
Origanum species

Oregano and wild marjoram are two names for *Origanum vulgare*, whose spicy aromatic leaves add zest to many meat and tomato dishes, and are an indispensable ingredient in Greek and Italian cuisines. The herb's various types of foliage and flowers also provide subtle ornament in the herb garden.

There are many other species of marjoram belonging to the *Origanum* genus, the more decorative of which can be used as edging plants or in mixed borders, where their attractive flower stems and aromatic leaves can be readily enjoyed. Some marjorams, including sweet marjoram (*O. majorana*), are half-hardy or tender – either grow them as annuals or protect them in winter.

Golden marjoram (*O. vulgare* 'Aureum') and gold-tipped marjoram (*O. vulgare* 'Gold Tip') provide wonderful splashes of colour in a herb garden. Golden marjoram has clusters of pretty tubular flowers in summer. Its foliage is a lemony-golden colour and makes a good display in the herb garden – but it should be planted in a semi-shady site to avoid leaf scorch from the sun. Gold-tipped marjoram has green leaves tipped with gold, and needs to be grown in a site that is not too shady or it will lose the variegation.

Sweet marjoram (*O. majorana*) forms a compact bushy plant, with a height and spread of about 30 cm (12 in). It needs protection in winter. Its foliage is good used fresh in cooking. Pot marjoram (*O. onites*) has pretty mauve flowers, is a bee-magnet and grows to a height of 45 cm (18 in).

For cooking, choose Greek oregano, or pot marjoram. The former keeps its flavour when dried, but the latter is better used fresh.

Of the several different forms of oregano or marjoram that can be used in cooking, the best is said to be Greek oregano (*O. vulgare* subsp. *hirtum*).

Some plants, including *O.* 'Kent Beauty' and *O. laevigatum* 'Herrenhausen', are generally regarded as decorative plants in the herb garden rather than for culinary use.

Cut back stems after flowering to encourage a flush of new foliage. You can lift and divide to make new plants in spring or autumn.

parsley
Petroselinum crispum

A basic herb of many cuisines, parsley is one of the main components of the *bouquet garni* herb bundle. You can use the leaves chopped up or whole in salads, as a garnish or as a flavouring for sauces and soups.

There are several varieties of curly-leaved parsley, with tightly curled moss-like leaves. All grow as low compact plants during their first year and flower in their second year. Also attractive, but much larger, is flat-leaved parsley – *Petroselinum crispum* 'Italian', or Italian or French parsley. It grows to a height of 30 cm (12 in). Its foliage is flat, and the stems and leaves are delicious either in salads or in cooked dishes.

Parsley is a hardy biennial that needs to be handled gently when it is transplanted because root disturbance will trigger its survival mechanism and set it in flowering mode too early. It prefers moisture-rich soil and partial shade. Buy plants in spring or autumn. Cover autumn-planted parsley with fleece or a cloche in winter to ensure a good supply of fresh herb.

The chopped leaves of parsley freeze well, and whole leaves can be dried for winter use. You can use parsley to make an alternative to Italian pesto sauce (usually made with basil), for parsley butter and in homemade cosmetics.

It is said that chewing parsley after drinking alcohol or eating garlic freshens the breath.

rosemary
Rosmarinus officinalis

The delicate flowers and strongly aromatic leaves of rosemary are ornamental in the herb garden and have long been valued as ingredients in cooking, herbal cosmetics and traditional remedies. The leaves can be dried or frozen for later use.

Rosemary has spiky aromatic leaves on woody branches. It is a hardy evergreen perennial in most areas, but may need protection in harsh winters. Upright forms can reach 2 m (6½ ft) in height, and the prostrate form spreads and trails. Harvest from growing tips to keep the plant bushy and encourage foliage production. Rosemary flowers in summer, with, depending on species and variety, small aromatic blooms in pink, white or blue.

Rosmarinus officinalis 'Prostratus' is a tender trailing or prostrate form with blue flowers. 'Albus' is hardy and has white flowers. For a tall rosemary hedge, choose 'Miss Jessopp's Upright'. 'Silver Spires' is a rediscovered rosemary that was popular in Tudor times; it has silvery variegated leaves and is attractive in any season. 'Majorcan Pink' is half hardy with pink flowers, while *R. lavandulaceus* is tender with blue flowers. 'Sudbury Blue' has delicate blue flowers.

This herb prefers a sunny site with a little protection from cold winter winds. Good drainage is essential. Remove any stems that die back in cold weather and cut back the plant to keep it in shape after flowering. Take cuttings in summer. Pick leaves when needed, but remember that the aromatic flavours are at their best before flowering. Whole stems or sprigs can be dried or frozen for later use. For drying in bulk, harvest in late summer.

Use rosemary flowers and chopped young leaves in salads. Sprigs of rosemary can be laid on joints of meat before roasting; the leaves are added to herb butters, jams, jellies and summer drinks, and are used to flavour sugar for desserts. Rosemary salt is good for seasoning meats and marinades. The herb is an ingredient of some homemade and proprietary skin cleansers and hair conditioners.

Part of the traditional *bouquet garni*, **parsley (left) is also a popular garnish, while rosemary (right) is a classic partner for lamb.**

sage
Salvia officinalis

Sage has been grown as a medicinal and culinary plant since ancient times. The name Salvia comes from the Latin word salvere, meaning to heal or save, and common sage – known for its astringent qualities – has been widely used as an antiseptic and cleansing herb in remedies and cosmetic preparations. Gargling with an infusion of sage can help to relieve the pain of a sore throat.

A hardy evergreen shrub with aromatic and decorative leaves, sage is as versatile in the kitchen as it is ornamental in the flower garden. It is used in numerous meat dishes, sometimes mixed with onion, and in salads, as well as in flavouring salt, oil and vinegar.

There are many sages that look decorative when used in the border, including *Salvia officinalis* 'Tricolor' with leaves variegated in purple, pink and white. Common sage has greyish-green leaves. Purple or red sage ('Purpurascens') has purple-grey leaves, while golden sage ('Icterina') has golden-green leaves.

Sages like full sun, an open site and light well-drained soil. Replace plants that become too woody. Take cuttings in spring or mid-autumn, or layer branches in situ. Common sage and its varieties can be grown from seed, sown direct into the growing site when danger of frost is past, or in seed trays, cells or plugs, where temperatures of 15–21°C (59–70°F) will ensure germination after two or three weeks.

If you are growing sage primarily for its leaves, cut out the flowering stems; pick leaves whenever you need them for cooking.

The classic herb for pork dishes, sage is often combined with apple sauce to form one of the best-known partnerships in English cuisine.

sorrel and buckler leaf sorrel

Rumex acetosa and *Rumex scutatus*

Sharp and clean to the taste, sorrel is an often undervalued element of the herb garden. Made into a sauce, it is a refreshing accompaniment to oily fish and adds piquancy to casseroles and stews. Buckler leaf sorrel (pictured), which has a milder taste, is particularly good in salads or as an alternative to spinach.

One of the traditional herbs of French cuisine, sorrel is a herbaceous perennial that, once established, will be in the herb garden for ever. It dies down in winter, but in spring its fresh green leaves appear – and at that time are at their tangy best for use in salads or sauces.

There are two sorrels that are useful in the kitchen and the garden. Common sorrel or garden sorrel (*R. acetosa*) is a strong-growing herb that makes large clumps of shield-shaped leaves, which should be eaten before the plant flowers; tall stems shoot up from the leaf mounds in summer, and the leaves on these stems do not taste as good. Small, unremarkable blooms are carried at the ends of the branched flower stems.

Of greater attraction in the garden is buckler leaf sorrel or French sorrel (*R. scutatus*). This comes in a green form and a more interesting silver-variegated form, 'Silver Shield', which has a marbled silvery centre to the leaf and gives good ground cover.

Sorrel is valued mainly for its culinary attributes, and has been used to treat blood disorders, but it has a high oxalic acid content and, if consumed in large quantities, may be harmful, especially to the kidneys – so use with caution.

Sorrel is one of the unsung treasures of the herb garden, especially when included in a sauce to serve with oily fish. Its tangy leaves can also be chewed to relieve thirst.

Tarragon
Artemisia dracunculus

The fiery aniseed flavour of tarragon makes it perfect for spicing meat and fish dishes. The leaves also add piquancy to oils and vinegars and are excellent in marinades. Pick the leaves during spring and summer to use fresh, and in late summer to freeze for winter use.

French tarragon is a hardy perennial with lance-like, narrow pale greenish-grey leaves. It can grow to a height of 90 cm (3 ft). In warm climates it may produce small flowers. In cold climates it doesn't flower and propagation is from stem cuttings in spring or root cuttings in autumn.

Grow tarragon in light well-drained soil in a sunny site, and cut it back in autumn. Protect the crown with a covering of conifer foliage or straw during winter. Divide plants in spring or autumn.

There is a less tasty but more vigorous form of the herb called Russian tarragon (*A. dracunculoides*), which is often sold wrongly labelled as French tarragon. This species is very hardy and will survive winters without protection, but it is worth growing French tarragon for its flavour, which is far superior to that of the Russian variety.

Although it has no modern medicinal uses, tarragon was once valued as an antidote to snake bites.

Tarragon packs a powerful punch in its narrow lance-like leaves. Often teamed with chicken, it is also the herb used to make sauce Béarnaise.

Thyme

Thymus vulgaris

An evergreen that can be used freshly picked all through the year, thyme is a component of *bouquet garni*. Both the flowers and the leaves are good in salads and are used to flavour oils, vinegars and marinades, as well as stocks and stews. Thyme is commonly added to stuffing for chickens. It combines particularly well with rosemary.

Thyme is a hardy evergreen sub-shrub with small, powerfully aromatic, spike-shaped or round leaves. There are variegated silver and golden forms.

The most vigorous and most useful for basic flavouring is common thyme (*T. vulgaris*), which has deep-green leaves and is a many-branched woody sub-shrub. It has mauve flowers. *T. vulgaris* 'Silver Posie' has silver variegated leaves and a good flavour. *T.* x *citriodorus* is a shrubby thyme, with small green lemon-scented leaves and pink flowers.

T. x *citriodorus* 'Silver Queen' is variegated with creamy silvery leaves, rosy-pink buds and a strong lemon scent to its leaves. *T. serpyllum* 'Snowdrift' is a creeping thyme that carpets the ground in white when in flower.

The herb is versatile, which means it can be grown equally well in the garden, on rockeries or in containers. The low-growing forms can be used to make attractive flowering paths or fragrant mats at the feet of benches. On a patio, plant up the cracks or gaps between paving slabs to make aromatic stepping stones.

Grow thyme in full sun in well-drained soil. After flowering, cut back the plant to promote new growth and bushy shapes. Replace plants every few years, when they become too woody and open at their centres.

Thyme has traditionally been used as an antiseptic.

Both upright and creeping forms of thyme produce aromatic leaves and attractive clusters of small pink, mauve or white flowers, which are as useful as the foliage in flavouring food.

gardening with herbs

how to grow herbs

Herbs are versatile plants that grow well in most types of garden soil and in most conditions. Their numbers can be increased by dividing plants or taking cuttings. Seed can often be sown direct into the ground – or you can sow it in pots and grow the new plants in windowsill propagation units or in a greenhouse.

Sow seed of hardy annuals direct into the soil in spring either in a seedbed or in their growing sites. Half-hardy herbs can also be sown in their growing sites once all danger of frost is past. Sow the seed in rows and just cover it with soil; water in well and thin out when seedlings are well established.

Sowing indoors produces plants ready for planting out as soon as the soil warms up and the seedlings have been hardened off in spring. Almost fill seed trays or cellular modules with soil, firm the surface down and water the compost or stand the trays in water. Leave the trays to drain before sowing fine seed into the compost surface. Space out large seeds and sieve a thin covering of compost over them. Put the trays in a heated propagator, with an even temperature of 15°C (59°F). Once the seeds have germinated and are large enough to handle,

transplant them into small individual pots. Harden off by leaving them outside during the day and returning them to the greenhouse at night, until they are acclimatized to outdoor conditions.

Before buying a herb that is ready to plant out in the garden or to grow indoors, check that it has no obvious disease or pest problems; avoid plants that are root-bound or have damaged stems. Plant out your new herb as soon as possible, but not during the hottest part of the day. Dig a hole large enough to take the rootball, and remove any weeds from the soil. Put the plant in the hole, backfill with soil, then firm the surface of the soil and water the plant well. In dry conditions water the plant daily until it is well established.

Evergreen herbs such as bay, rosemary, sage and thyme can be harvested from outdoor and indoor herb collections all year, as can herbs that you have forced into growth in winter, such as mint, tarragon and chives. Annual herbs, including basil, perilla, rocket, dill, nasturtium and coriander/cilantro, are at their best in spring and summer – late summer in the case of basil. Since herbaceous perennial herbs including

LEFT **Use sharp clean scissors to harvest herb flowers such as those of lavender. Cut low down on the stem, so that you have long stems to tie into bundles for drying. Harvest on dry days, when the sun has just burnt off the dew and before it gets too hot. Lay the harvested material into a trug or basket and keep it in the shade until you are ready to use it. Harvest only the amount that you can work with in a short time, or the flowers may begin to deteriorate and wilt.**

SEQUENCE STARTING FROM TOP LEFT
Put a label in place before you sow. Empty the seed packet into your hand and then take a pinch of seed, or one seed if they are large, and place it in the trench or hole. Just cover the soil and firm it down with the back of your hand. Mark the line of the row with a trail of coloured gravel, especially if sowing parsley, which is notoriously slow to germinate.

fennel, lovage and comfrey die back in winter, their harvest period is during the spring and summer.

When each plant has produced good leafy growth, harvest it in an even way, to maintain a well-defined shape. For a handful of leaves to add to salads or cooked dishes, pick the herbs just before you want them, at any time of day.

To promote the vigorous growth of your herbs or to increase their numbers, divide the plants in early spring when they are still dormant, or in autumn when the growing season is coming to an end. In autumn, before dividing, cut back all the spent flowering stems. Then use a fork to lever the clump

out of the ground. When it is loosened, lift it out and place it on the soil surface.

The traditional way to divide large plants is to place two forks back to back in the centre of the clump and prise the two sections of the plant apart. Keep on doing this to each section until you have reduced the size of the original clump and produced several new sections ready for replanting. Herbs such as chives can be prised apart by hand. Most perennials, such as marjoram, chives, echinacea, tarragon, sorrel, creeping thyme and lovage, grow to form large basal clumps. The growth at the centre becomes weak, and leaf production usually declines.

gardening with herbs **33**

When the clump is divided, any unhealthy-looking sections can be discarded, which allows the new plant or division to grow healthy new shoots from the rootstock around its edge.

By taking cuttings from individual plants you can produce many new plants for your herb garden. You can use a cutting to reproduce exactly the plant from which you have taken the cutting.

To take a softwood cutting, start by looking for strong and healthy new shoots as soon as the herbs begin to grow in spring. Cut them away from the parent plant with a sharp knife and, if you are taking several cuttings, put them in a plastic bag to keep them moist and cool, and to prevent them from wilting. Prepare several pots or trays with a good, well-drained cuttings compost. Make a clean cut on the stem of each cutting just below a leaf node, so that each is 10 cm (4 in) long. Cut the lower leaves

off each cutting, but leave a few leaves on the stem. Make holes in the compost with a dibber, and put the cuttings in the holes up to the level of the remaining leaves.

Label each cutting with name and date, then put the pot of cuttings in a heated propagator or a mini-greenhouse made of a plastic bag. Check the cuttings daily; if using a plastic bag, take it off and turn it inside out every day.

When roots start to appear on the underside of the pot – between a fortnight and four weeks – begin to apply a foliar feed. When the plants are large enough, pot them on into individual pots. Pinch out the growing tips of leafy shoots to encourage a bushy habit.

The method for taking hardwood cuttings is similar to that for taking softwood ones, but hardwood cuttings prefer a very well-drained compost and, since they are taken later in the year – in autumn, when the stems are hard and woody – they need to be overwintered in cold frames or greenhouses before they can be planted out the following autumn. The rooting time for hardwood cuttings is much longer than for softwood cuttings.

A simple way to propagate or increase herbs is to take root cuttings in spring or autumn from healthy-looking plants. Mint, bergamot, lemon balm,

SEQUENCE FROM LEFT **Unless they are in a very large and congested clump, chives can easily be divided by hand. Dig up and divide the clump into smaller sections by gently pulling it apart. Discard dead or damaged material. Replant smaller sections in prepared planting holes. Backfill and firm in soil at the surface. Trim the tops of the newly divided plants and water them. Keep the row weed-free and in a short time you will have a crop of fresh chives.**

horseradish, comfrey and sweet woodruff are among the herb plants that can be increased in this way.

Unless they are grown in crowded situations where there is no free circulation of air, or the plants are kept either too wet or too dry, herbs usually remain free of pests and diseases. It is preferable to use organic methods rather than proprietary insecticides or fungicides to deter pests from food plants such as herbs. Many organic gardeners use a proprietary organic soap to make a soapy liquid to use on whitefly or greenfly infestations. Brown spots on mint and chive foliage are symptoms of a disease called mint or onion rust. Plants that are badly affected should be dug up and removed from the herb garden, so that other plants are not infected. You can also sterilize the soil around mint plants to prevent this disease from occurring: place a layer of straw around the affected plant and set the straw alight – but take great care to ensure that the fire does not spread.

Seedlings of basil and other herbs are prone to damping off and dying in the early stages of growth. Deterrents include good air circulation, hygienic conditions, judicious watering, and drenching the compost with a fungicidal compound before sowing.

Scale insects may be a problem on the evergreen leaves of bay grown in containers indoors. Use a soapy liquid to wipe the leaves, and dislodge the scale insects with the head of a cotton bud.

Vine weevil, whitefly and red spider mites may be persistent in protected environments, but can be controlled using soapy sprays or biological controls. Eelworms or nematodes are used for vine weevil, a parasitic wasp called *Encarsia* formosa for whitefly, and *Phytoseiulus persimilis* for red spider mites.

Many herbs self-seed abundantly. Others can be increased by dividing clumps, taking cuttings or sowing fresh seed in spring.

beautiful borders

Many of the plants categorized as herbs are attractive flowering or foliage plants that can be taken out of the context of the herb garden and used successfully in a mixed border.

Sage – whose foliage colours range from silver to purple, and include a tricolour variety that is grey-green with hints of pink and white – is a particularly effective border plant. It grows to form a low mass of coloured foliage, so it can be useful at the base of plants such as roses that may have bare stems. Later in the season, when in flower itself, sage offers extra ornament. Once the flowers are over, cut back the plant to prevent it from becoming leggy and out of shape and to encourage continuous foliage production.

If you have space to accommodate their invasive habits, herbs such as mint, comfrey and sweet Cicely will provide good-textured, colourful and shapely foliage followed by pretty flowers. All three are useful in shady sites, with mint being suited to moister conditions. Borage is another vigorous but useful foliage plant that bears eye-catching blue or white flowers in summer.

Heartsease, with its small mauve faces, is useful in containers as well as at the front of a border, winding its way through other plants. Their silver foliage and dainty pink or white scented blooms make pinks suitable for low-growing at the front of the border. Similarly, thyme will provide variegated gold or silver foliage, delicate white, mauve or pink blooms and, in some cases, a low-growing mat-like habit.

Oregano or marjoram is a rewarding herb for the middle or front of a flower border, and will grow to form quite large clumps of flowering stems in white or mauve.

Most herb flowers are in the mauve, pink or white ranges, but plants such as fennel, pot marigold, with its sunny orange and creamy yellow flowers, and nasturtium, in shades of orange, cream and red, provide

ABOVE LEFT **Mauve marjoram graces the front of a border, while evening primrose, chicory and fennel offer tall stems of flowers in yellow and blue, white or (in some species of chicory) pink, which seem to float high in the air.**

BELOW LEFT **Star-like blue chicory looks lovely en masse, as well as in a mixed planting.**

RIGHT **Lavender and curry plant grow in curved shapes, which makes their silver-grey foliage useful for softening the edges of borders.**

great swathes of colour in the mixed border. Nasturtium has the added advantage of colourful foliage and looks good weaving its way along the front of the border. St John's wort can be used to add spots of buttery yellow to the front of the border, complementing evening primrose in a similar shade at the back; both herbs will self-seed copiously, so cut them back once the blooms are spent.

At a slightly higher level, fennel's early offering to the border is a froth of fern-like foliage in either green or bronze, followed by stiff upside-down umbrella-like flower heads with masses of small yellow dot-like flowers. These are a magnet for beneficial garden insects such as hoverflies, and, since fennel self-seeds abundantly around the garden, at the height of summer it offers great stands of colour, seemingly dancing with life.

Lavender, pinks and some other herbs grow in soft mounded shapes that spill over the border's edge. Others, such as chicory, offer flowering stems that seem to float through other plants in the border. Rosemary and bay are useful grown as standards in formal gardens, serving to raise eye-level and to make a repeated theme along a long border.

In late summer, traditional herb-garden plants, such as echinacea, or purple coneflower (also available in a white and a green form), are especially useful because they flower over a long period late in the season. Bergamot, or monarda, has a similarly long and late flowering season, and provides tall stems of flowers arranged in whorls of mauve, white and pink around its square stems. Agastache, with mauve-and-white flower spikes, is also useful for the middle of the late summer border.

LEFT **Echinacea, or purple coneflower, is a native American herb with a long medicinal tradition. It has many potential uses in modern medicine, and is constantly being assessed for its benefits to the human immune system. In the flower border it offers attractive long-lasting blooms late in the season.**

ABOVE RIGHT **Box trained into formal shapes is a useful accent in a mixed border. Bergamot, or monarda, and marjoram bring a lovely combination of foliage and flowers to the border.**

BELOW RIGHT **Pot marigolds will brighten a sunny border in spring and early summer. To encourage a continuity of flowering, remove the spent flowers before they set seed.**

covering the ground

Many low-growing herbs can be effective in the ornamental garden as ground-covering plants. Creeping thyme, for example, makes a flat green mat of foliage, and in summer offers its small mauve blooms for extra show. In a border it hugs the ground at the feet of taller plants, suppressing weeds and providing its own colour. Deadhead thyme after flowering, using shears or clippers. Remove any weed seedlings that grow through the ground cover and water it in dry spells.

Since it supports light trampling underfoot, thyme can be used for a short path. More formally, it makes a witty and attractive feature if planted in a circle at the base of a sundial. You can also use a slightly taller thyme for an inner circle within the creeping thyme outer circle, adding contrast to the colour and texture of the ground cover.

Creeping chamomile is also useful as a fragrant ground cover, to create an aromatic lawn or as a pathway plant. Remove all perennial weeds and any stones from the soil before planting. For 1 square metre (1 square yard), you will need 40 individual chamomile plants. Water the plants in well, and avoid walking on the path or lawn until they are well established and have meshed together.

ABOVE AND LEFT **Creeping thyme (above) or chamomile (left) wears better when grown in between stepping stones. Either herb supports light traffic and provides a highly aromatic pathway to a bench or an arbour. Both need clipping back to stop them covering the stepping stones.**

ABOVE **Two types of thyme form the ground cover that frames pots holding lemon verbena and an ornamental garden plant, Perovskia 'Blue Spire'.**

Either thyme or chamomile makes a fragrant cover for a turf seat or bench. Site the seat against an existing wall and make a back for it with trellis or wood. You can build up the seat in front of it as you would a raised bed, using smaller raised beds to form the 'arms' of the seat. Plant the creeping herbs in the soil within the various raised areas and, if you are using trellis for the back, plant a climber such as jasmine into the bed, for fragrance in the air and at your back.

Prostrate rosemary, although it is slower growing than thyme and chamomile, and also tender in cold areas, is effective both as a ground cover and trailing over the edges of beds. Plant in full sun.

Corsican mint, *Mentha requienii,* won't support feet, but it does make a good cover at the edge of a pond or in a moist, shady conditions. Similarly, creeping mint, *M. pulegium*, is attractive in a shady, slightly damp area of the garden. Herbs such as *Alchemilla mollis*, sweet Cicely and salad burnet, although not ground-hugging, are useful ground-cover plants in a large garden. As they self-seed abundantly, their spread can be prodigious.

gardening with herbs **41**

a hedge of herbs

Rosemary, thyme, santolina, box and lavender are among the herbs that can be grown as shaped low hedges to enclose formal features or even to form the fabric of herb parterres. Herb hedges are usually shaped to make linear ribbons of foliage that outline or emphasize special areas of a herb garden. Yew may be slow-growing, but once it is established it is a very elegant dark-green foil for herbs, and in the general garden it is particularly useful as an architectural hedge plant.

Knot gardens and parterres are the usual formal features created with herb plants. The colour of the hedge depends on the plants you choose for it. For a silvery effect, use lavender or santolina or even curry plant. Thyme, rosemary and box provide green elements, and by mixing the silver and greens you can create a woven effect.

Although you can achieve a formal effect by keeping lavender closely clipped, you can also create a relaxed and informal look by allowing it to flower in summer, then cutting it back once the flowering is finished. A lavender hedge makes an attractive feature on either side of a pathway, but remember to make the path wide enough to allow the lavender spikes to spill across it and yet leave enough space for you to walk along.

In a vegetable garden use parsley, wild strawberries or chives to edge part of the garden. This will provide an informal and semi-permanent hedge, which will alter as you harvest from it.

When you plant a herb hedge use plants of the same height and size so that you achieve a uniform look more quickly. Plant box or yew into individual planting holes along a line of string. Water the plants in well and, if necessary, provide a temporary windbreak of hessian to help the young plants survive in their first winter.

When the hedge is well established, you can begin to clip it to maintain it. Cut back knot-garden or parterre hedges in early autumn, so that there is time for them to recover before the cold weather sets in. Woody plants such as sage, thyme, lavender and rosemary should be cut back to half the year's growth to promote bushy shapes. For extra effect, cut special shapes, such as triangles, globes or even whimsical animals or birds, into the hedges.

OPPOSITE PAGE **A circle of wall germander, or *Teucrium chamaedrys*, is created from single plants of the same size planted to a particular design then cut back annually to form the desired shape.**

ABOVE **Cotton lavender or santolina can be grown to achieve a silvery effect.**

BELOW **After it has finished flowering, cut back the lavender to a uniform height for a fragrant hedge.**

gardening with herbs **43**

herbs in the kitchen garden

Growing popular culinary herbs such as parsley and chives as crops in the vegetable garden means you can harvest from several plants at the same time rather than from one or two – so that each plant loses some of its foliage, flowers or seeds, but enough remains for the plant to continue to be decorative and viable.

Group tall-growing plants such as fennel and lovage together and plant them at the back of the vegetable garden so that they don't cast shade on or take light away from lower-growing herbs. Low-growing herbs such as parsley, salad burnet, chives and buckler leaf sorrel look attractive in short rows in raised beds.

Sow parsley in succession through the summer so that you have a number of rows at different stages. Once parsley begins to send up a strong, tough flowering stem its foliage becomes less aromatic, and you should uproot the plants. If you have an informal vegetable garden, allow one to flower and set seed, and then to self-seed.

Summer savory, an annual with tasty edible flowers and foliage, has traditionally been cooked and served with broad beans; it is also often used as a companion plant for broad beans in the vegetable garden. Another good companion herb is sweet Cicely, traditionally linked with one of the early fruits

of the productive garden, rhubarb. Use its leafy shoots to sweeten and reduce the acidity of rhubarb. Sweet Cicely self-sows copiously, so remove its seeds once they have formed or harvest them to use as aniseed-flavoured sweets.

Mint is an invaluable kitchen herb, useful in salads and in cooked dishes, sauces and jams and jellies. It is a vigorous plant, and is best grown in containers sunk into the ground, or in a section of the vegetable garden that can be cordoned off from the rest of the rows. Although its flowers are attractive, keep cutting out flowering stems to encourage more leafy shoots.

Cut back thyme and sage after flowering to promote the growth of new leafy shoots. Rosemary also benefits from cutting back. Some woody herbs become leggy and unshapely in time. If this happens, replace them with new plants.

Grow golden marjoram and chervil in relative shade in the vegetable garden. Chervil is a biennial producing leafy growth in its first year, so make successive sowings to keep your kitchen supplied with its subtle flavours.

Herbs such as nasturtium, heartsease and pot marigold provide edible flowers for use in salads. Chive flower heads are also good in salads – pick them just as the buds begin to open.

Shrubby herbs such as rosemary, sage and thyme need extra space in the vegetable garden, but you are unlikely to need more than one or two of each to support your cooking needs.

ABOVE Confine vigorous mint (left) in a restricted area of the kitchen garden. Rosemary (centre) can be clipped into shapes or allowed to grow freely. Use flat-leaved parsley (right) as a seasonal edging.

BELOW Harvest the aromatic seeds of caraway (left) after the flowers die back. Mossy curly-leaved parsley (centre) can also be used as a temporary edging. The flowers, foliage and seeds of nasturtium (right) are spicy in food – and it will romp through the vegetable garden, providing annual colour.

creating a herb collection

If you have space to grow herbs for ornament, display them in groups according to their use or to show the differences between plants in the same genus. There are herbs for every theme and colour scheme. For example, collections of mint, rosemary, thyme, sage, lavender and marjoram reveal a wide range of foliage colour, flower colour and, in many cases, essential oils and aromas. Such collections, arranged by genus and species, show the characteristics of the various plants and display the differences between each species and form.

Before you plant a collection you need to know the maximum heights and spreads of the various plants and how much sun they need. Look at the different foliage colours and place them so that they look good together.

The simplest collection consists of the herbs you use often in the kitchen. Grow them in a small circular bed or in containers close to the kitchen door, for easy access. You could devote a small rectangular bed to bay, thyme and parsley, the three classic herbs of a *bouquet garni*. Choose a standard or conical-shaped bay as the central focus. Plant thyme bushes in the corners of the bed, and fill the centre with parsley. For a *fines herbes* collection, grow parsley, chervil, chives and tarragon.

BELOW LEFT **Mints are best grown in individual pots to prevent these vigorous plants from overwhelming each other.**

BELOW CENTRE **Marjoram and summer savoy reveal a wide range of foliage colour and flower colour.**

BELOW RIGHT **Rosemary flowers can be white, pink, mauve or blue. Most species are medium-height, but 'Miss Jessopp's Upright', which can grow to 2.5 m (8 ft), needs to be carefully sited in such a collection, as does prostrate or creeping rosemary.**

OPPOSITE PAGE **A circle is a popular shape for a basic culinary collection containing herbs such as rosemary, chives, marjoram and buckler leaf sorrel.**

If you like Italian cuisine, grow bay, basil, marjoram, garlic, rosemary and sage. For an Asian taste, choose coriander/cilantro, lemon grass, Japanese parsley, perilla and mint. Pizza herb gardens containing marjoram, basil and rosemary are popular in the USA.

You could also group together herbs whose leaves are used dried or fresh to make teas and tisanes, such as sage, mint, bergamot and chamomile. Other possibilities include fragrant herbs for a potpourri collection, and an edible flower collection. Enjoy cowslip and violet flowers crystallized or baked in cakes and scones. Use pot marigold, chive and thyme flowers fresh in salads. Lavender flowers and rose petals added to ordinary or caster/superfine sugar will transform it into a scented sweetener for baking and desserts.

The many herbs that have citrus-scented foliage would make an attractive collection with their differing heights, shapes, foliage and flower colours. Such plants include variegated lemon balm, lemon verbena, lemon thyme and some tender herbs such as lemon-scented basil, lemon grass and *Eucalyptus citriodora*.

BELOW **Edging an informal path with collections of marjoram and catmint offers a flowing, curving shape to the garden and displays differences in flower colour.**

LEFT **A number of different thyme species are grown within a small parterre or knot garden, hedged in by rosemary, box and a golden form of the honeysuckle *Lonicera nitida*, 'Baggessen's Gold', a shrubby hedge plant.**

gardening with herbs **49**

herbs in containers

Many low-growing or trailing herbs grow well in containers, and containers make it easy to ring the changes and replace spent herbs quickly as you use particular plants or different varieties become available during the season.

The most convenient containers for kitchen herbs are window boxes placed just outside the kitchen, so that you can harvest foliage and flowers easily and quickly without having to step outside, or large ground-level containers on a patio.

If any of the herbs in a container dies, or you harvest them so completely that they are no longer attractive, it is simple to remove and replace them. In addition, if you are going to be using and replacing the herbs regularly, you can leave them in their individual containers, all set into a sturdy wooden window box, with the box becoming a cachepot for the various smaller containers. You can replace any herb that is not growing well without having to replant the whole box.

There is a range of different containers that are suitable for herb growing. Terracotta and plastic are popular choices, but you can use almost anything, from large olive-oil cans to half-barrels, to create a particular style and house your herb collection.

There are two things you need to be sure of when planting up a container with herbs. First, it should have a depth of at least 25–30 cm (10–12 in), to give the roots adequate space to make strong root runs. Second, larger containers are heavy to move once they are filled with moist compost, so you need to site them carefully before you plant them up. If you are planting up a window box or hanging basket, make sure that it is securely fixed in position. When it is full of moist soil it will be very heavy, and if it became unsecured it could fall and hurt someone passing underneath it, especially if you happen to live in an apartment.

LEFT **Terracotta pots are attractive containers for herbs because they weather so well. Annual herbs and some perennials, including chives, thrive in small pots in the short term. Woody perennials such as sage and thyme need relatively deep pots so that their roots can get properly established.**

Remove the individual herbs from their pots and
place them on a drainage layer of broken terracotta
and a layer of soil-based compost. Fill the spaces
between the herbs with compost and firm the plants
in with your hands. Water the soil and cover its
surface with a layer of grit to hold the compost in
place and to act as a water-absorbent mulch.

There are a number of herbs that will thrive
growing together in a container in a sunny
situation. Avoid tall-growing plants – especially for
a window box where the window opens outwards
– because they will flop over the edge and may be
damaged by wind.

*Low-growing or trailing herbs and stately
standards make a fine display in containers.*

OPPOSITE, FAR LEFT **Standard bay trees make strong focal points in a formal herb garden. In winter, insulate the pot with bubble wrap to prevent frost damage and stablize it so that it doesn't blow over.**

OPPOSITE, CENTRE AND RIGHT **Weathered stone sinks or sculpted terracotta pots are practical and attractive containers for shrubby herbs such as sage. They are also suitable for low-growing collections of creeping and upright thymes.**

ABOVE **A bold and flamboyant display in a container can be used as a marker for the meeting point of paths or to provide a change of height in the low-growing herb garden.**

growing herbs indoors

Many herbs can be grown indoors all year round, but indoor herbs are particularly useful in winter for quick harvesting. In sheltered sites they can also be grown on patios and balconies throughout the winter.

It is advisable to treat indoor herbs as practical or useful plants with short shelf or windowsill lives rather than as long-lived plants. In common with other container-grown plants, they need nutrients, water, protection from pests, adequate light and free circulation of air.

A kitchen windowsill is usually the most suitable site for herbs in pots because it is convenient for the cook and is likely to have good light and air circulation. Choose attractive containers for extra decorative effect, or group together several herbs in larger containers to create a mini-herb garden indoors.

As a general rule, herbs should be grown in separate pots in well-drained compost. This allows easy replacement of dead or overharvested herbs. Water the plants regularly, but in winter keep rosemary, sage, winter savory and thyme just moist.

Herbs grown indoors in summer need a liquid feed every two to three weeks – or add a slow-release fertilizer pellet to the compost when you pot the plants up. Use a spray of insecticidal soap to kill off any whitefly; spray every 14 days until the infestation has abated.

Harvest the herbs as required, but turn each plant every few days to encourage even leafy growth and to help you to harvest evenly from it. If you overharvest from one plant it will look less attractive and may become more vulnerable to pests and diseases. For quick results, replace indoor plants with new ones bought from supermarkets; for a longer growing period, replace them with herbs from garden centres. You can sow parsley and chervil in succession to provide new material.

Evergreen herbs such as rosemary, sage and thyme can be grown indoors, but they are best suited to outdoor growing. Annuals such as basil and parsley last for a short time, but replacement pots can be bought regularly from supermarkets for immediate use.

If you have no garden and are growing herbs in pots indoors all year round, repot evergreen perennials annually in spring. The plants may need replacing every two or three years. Plants such as fennel and dill, which would normally grow very tall outdoors, should be harvested when they are reasonably short, or the plant will become leggy and look untidy and out of line with its windowsill companions.

If you have a heated greenhouse, you can force tarragon, mint and chives into growing during what is normally their dormant season. Pot them up in autumn and keep them in the greenhouse through the winter, planting them out into the garden in spring.

Container herbs can be bought from supermarkets at any time of the year to fill the flavour gap between your own sowings and provide leaves for salads and cooked dishes. The hot-house conditions in which they are grown are difficult to replicate in the average draughty kitchen, but you can prolong their lives by keeping them out of draughts, watering them from the base and harvesting them evenly. Even if you are careful with them, it is unlikely that supermarket plants will become long-term inhabitants of your indoor collection. In some circles they are known as 'cut-and-chuck' herbs because of their short-term use.

Supermarkets can also be a source of unusual herbs for indoors. For example, lemon grass plants can be grown from stems bought in supermarket packs. (In some Oriental supermarkets they are sold loose.) Choose the plumpest stem and check that it has not been sliced at the base. Plant the stem into a gritty compost and keep it on the dry side during winter. Alternatively, good-sized plants are available from specialist herb growers and will provide citrus-scented foliage much earlier than the supermarket stems.

Herbs in the kitchen are a boon to the cook, but they need a light and airy site to thrive.

FROM LEFT **Fennel, parsley, basil and sage will grow well on a sunny windowsill but should be kept out of draughts. Fennel tends to become leggy if grown indoors in a container, so use it quickly.**

gardening with herbs **55**

living with herbs

To create a warm welcome, bring the essence of a summer garden indoors with a potpourri of flowers, herbs and spices.

The original 'rotten pot' that gave us the word potpourri was a wet mixture of fermented petals and leaves. Today, the dry potpourri is more popular. Its scent may not last as long as that of the moist variety, but the combinations of textures, colours and aromas are endless. The basic ingredients are flowers for scent or colour, aromatic leaves, peel and spices, and a fixative – usually powdered orris root – to preserve the blend. Use 1 tablespoon of orris root for each cupped handful of dried flowers and leaves; then add a few drops of essential oils, if desired.

ABOVE AND OPPOSITE PAGE **For a zesty hallway, add essential oils of bergamot, grapefruit and lemon to a bowl of dried lemon balm, lemon verbena, mint, yellow rosebuds and citrus slices. Any essential oil must be used sparingly or it will drown the subtler scents of the leaves and petals. The potpourri in this shallow bowl – about the size of a standard dinner plate – needs no more than 2 drops of each oil.**

RIGHT **If you want to enhance the rustic feel in a room with plenty of wooden furniture, mix 2 or 3 drops of essential oils of pine, sandalwood and cedar with large handfuls of dried rose petals, bay leaves and lavender sprigs, along with generous sprinklings of ground cinnamon and nutmeg.**

Designed for comfort and entertaining, living rooms are full of soft furnishings and display surfaces that offer a host of opportunities for scenting and decorating with herbs.

A simple way to scent your home is to have arrangements of fresh flowers and herbs in every room, but there are other, more imaginative ways to keep it smelling delicious and inviting all year round.

For example, herb sachets – which have traditionally been used to freshen drawers and linen cupboards – can also be tucked into cushions, into the pockets of everyday coats and clothes, and down the sides of comfy chairs and sofas. Fragrances are released when herb-filled cushions are pressed or leant against; curtain hems can be filled with dried aromatic herbs, or fresh lavender sprigs can simply be tucked into muslin/gauze curtains. Experiment with different mixtures of dried herbs and essential oils to make a potpourri, perhaps combining it with a pomander. Circulating air will pick up and mingle these scents, so ensure that the various fragrances are complementary, and there is no clash of pungent odours.

For a sweet aroma, choose from herbs that sweeten, which include bay, lavender, lemon verbena, rosemary, santolina, myrtle, thyme and sweet woodruff.

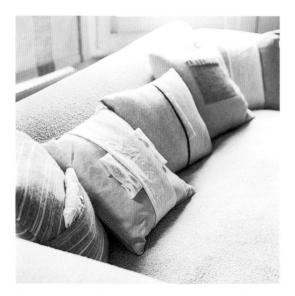

ABOVE **For a heady, long-lasting winter fragrance, press cloves into oranges to make pomanders. Display several in a dish with a selection of herbs and spices such as bay, eucalyptus, juniper berries and cinnamon.**

LEFT AND OPPOSITE PAGE **Herb sachets can be a decorative element in themselves, while subtly perfuming an entire room – the perfect setting in which to enjoy a cup of chamomile tea.**

pocketing a subtle perfume

A pocket in a cushion invites you to fill it with herbs. Herbs that are good for this purpose include eucalyptus (opposite page), rosemary and bay leaves. For a mixture of herbs, whole or crushed, cut a square of muslin/cheesecloth and fold it to make an envelope around the herbs (this page). Wrap a band of linen around a cushion, securing the ends with a button or a stitch. Tuck the folded muslin sachet under the band. Essential oils sprinkled on the muslin/cheesecloth bag enhance and prolong the fragrance.

BELOW **You can buy ready-scented beeswax candles, or add essential oils or small pieces of dried herb to melted beeswax while making your own. Tied up in ribbon with lavender sprigs, these make beautiful home-made Christmas presents.**

A handful of woody sprigs on a log fire sweetens the smoky aromas of winter.

ABOVE AND LEFT **If you have a log fire, throw on a handful of woody-stemmed herbs every so often to release the rich aromas. Layering logs with branches of rosemary both looks pretty and complements the woody smells.**

Burning woody herbs such as rosemary, lavender and bay will fill a room with rich musty aromas. Either keep a box of dried herbs by an open fire to use as kindling, or throw an occasional handful on the embers. Logs stored in the home can be layered with generous sprigs of rosemary (drying the rosemary beforehand should stop it going black). Another delicious winter fragrance is the smell of burning candles. To create your own herbal version, buy a candlemaking kit. Just before pouring the melted wax into moulds, add small pieces of dried herb, such as bergamot, wall germander, lavender heads, lemon thyme, mint, rosemary or myrtle, or a few drops of essential oil of your choice.

living with herbs **65**

A flamboyant winter wreath creates a Yuletide mood.

OPPOSITE PAGE AND LEFT **A wreath of pine branches, eucalyptus, rosemary, bay, slices of dried citrus fruit, and bundles of cinnamon sticks will fill a room with a distinctively festive mixture of colours, textures and fragrances.**

One of the most traditional ways of using herbs for decoration is to weave them into a wreath. This adds fragrance and colour to a room and, if used imaginatively, can become the central focus. The wreath shown is a strong enough statement to be the only festive decoration in the room.

To make a wreath, use plain wire, moss-covered wire or willow, and secure into a hoop. (Or buy a hoop ready-made at any florist's shop.) Using thin wire, attach bunches of selected herbs. For the main body of the wreath, use branches of pine, eucalyptus, bay and rosemary, then carefully tuck in among the branches slices of dried oranges, lemons and limes, fresh or dried Chinese lanterns and bundles of cinnamon sticks. For the final festive touch, add bunches of red berries.

If the wreath is to hang horizontally, attach it to a strong structure such as the iron candelabra illustrated. When it is time to take down the wreath, burn the bunches of herbs on an open fire and enjoy the powerful aroma.

FAR LEFT **To dry herbs, tie a few sprigs together and hang them in a warm, dark room.**

LEFT **Herb oils and vinegars should be stored in airtight bottles out of direct sunlight.**

RIGHT **Hanging herbs from the ceiling can produce a dramatic decorative effect. Bunches of sage, lemon balm, rosemary and eucalyptus, dried or fresh, will brighten up any kitchen.**

The medieval still room for processing and preserving herbs has long since disappeared from the home. Such activities are now likely to take place in the kitchen, where herbs may also be stored, grown (see pages 54–55) or – as in other rooms – used decoratively.

As soon as possible after harvesting or buying herbs, put them in water and out of direct sunlight. To revive cooking herbs that are starting to wilt, put them in a plastic bag filled with air and secure it tightly; stored in the refrigerator, they should last a few extra days.

The sooner after harvesting that the drying process begins the better the quality and colour of the dried herbs, but drying cannot be rushed because moisture must be removed gradually from a plant. Wipe off any soil or grit but avoid washing the leaves. Choose a warm, dry, dark place with good ventilation, such as an airing cupboard or a heated loft or attic. Hang several sprigs of each herb in separate small bunches, tied loosely with string or raffia, so that the air can get in and around each bunch. Leave herbs hanging, stems upwards, for about a week, until the leaves are paper-dry and fragile but not disintegrating. Remove leaves from stems, keeping them whole, and store in airtight bottles away from sunlight. Check dried leaves regularly for moisture, mould and insects, and throw them away if you find anything wrong. Most dried herbs will last for about a year.

Freezing is a good way to retain the colour and flavour of delicate herbs such as basil, chives, dill and tarragon. Before freezing, wipe the herbs and pack them into labelled plastic food bags or boxes.

Generous bunches of dried herbs, or herbs preserved in attractive bottles of oil or vinegar, can be used in the kitchen for decorative as well as culinary purposes.

RIGHT **The acrid smell of rue repels flies and ants. Hang up bunches of the herb in utility rooms to discourage infestations, and press the leaves occasionally to release their pungent scent.**

BELOW **Pretty posies of santolina in your linen drawers will ward off the dreaded moth.**

RIGHT **To make your wooden furniture smell dreamy, add a few drops of essential oil of lavender to a good-quality beeswax furniture polish, and apply with a clean dry cloth.**

BELOW **To give a wonderfully fresh fragrance to floors and surfaces, clean them with 6 drops of an essential oil added to 2 litres/8 cups of warm water. Choose from oils of lemon, tea tree, thyme, lavender, sandalwood, peppermint and eucalyptus.**

Herbal preparations have a multitude of practical uses in the home – and they are frequently kinder to your skin and the environment than chemical-based cleaners.

Herbs have always had an important practical role in the household, and that remains true today – indeed, incorporating herbs or essential herbal oils in your cleaning routine can make household chores an aromatic pleasure. You can use them to disinfect floors and surfaces, to repel unwanted visitors such as moths and other insects, and to sweeten and purify stale, musty air.

Ants are seen off by sprigs of pennyroyal, rue and tansy left on larder shelves. Rue also deters flies, as do lavender, mint, mugwort, pennyroyal and peppermint. Use the herbs dried in potpourri, or fresh in arrangements and wreaths. Make sure that the leaves are disturbed occasionally to release more scent. To prevent unwelcome visits from weevils, place a few bay leaves in bins of flour, rice and dried pulses.

living with herbs **71**

ABOVE **Roses, pelargoniums and Chinese lanterns add colour to a summer garland of flat-leaved parsley, bay, lemon balm, coriander/ cilantro, fennel, apple mint, eucalyptus and sage.**

RIGHT **As well as making flamboyant centrepieces, fresh herbs can be used for plate decorations, in finger bowls and in place-marker pots.**

FAR RIGHT **Leaves of borage and mint with cucumber slices make iced water even more refreshing. Coriander/ cilantro flowers impart a delicate flavour to pepper and salt.**

Decorating a summer table with fresh herbs is a joy in itself. There is such a wide choice of plants and flowers available in summer that each detail can be a celebration of a different herb. For example, wrapping flowering rosemary around napkins will encourage your guests to appreciate the plant's delicate purple flower.

For your tablecloth, choose a pale natural fabric such as undyed linen. This will allow the herbs to hold centre stage rather than making them compete with a busy pattern. Height is important in any table setting, and one easy way to achieve it is to decorate candlesticks or candelabra. Soak a foam brick in water. (These can be bought in any florist's shop and, if kept damp, will maintain the freshness of the herbs for days.) Slice off two chunks, one for each side of the candlestick, and use florist's tape to wrap them together. Rosemary, eucalyptus, lemon balm, parsley, flowering apple mint and various pelargoniums make a good base. You can then introduce more delicate herbs and flowers

Intensify the pleasures of summer dining by combining the delicate scents of freshly cut flowers and herbs with the stronger aromas of herbs used in cookery and the spicy flavours of salad herbs.

ABOVE LEFT **A sprig of rosemary tied loosely around a crisp linen napkin is a pretty alternative to a napkin ring.**

ABOVE RIGHT **The woody stems of lemon balm are easily woven into lattice-pattern place mats. When a hot plate is placed on a mat, a delicious aroma is released.**

such as flowering coriander/cilantro and old-fashioned scented roses. Combining culinary herbs and scent-giving herbs in a table decoration can produce very satisfying results, especially if the culinary herbs have also been used in the preparation of food. As with the tablecloth, choose plain or understated china, cutlery and glassware that will not upstage the greenery. Arrange the herbs loosely;

think about how they grow in the garden and let them ramble across the table. Herbs wilt quickly, so make sure they are in plenty of water. Spray loose herbs with water half an hour before your guests sit down, to keep the table looking fresh.

A bowl of freshly torn herbs such as basil, mint, tarragon, coriander/cilantro and flat-leaved parsley is an attractive detail – and guests can help themselves to handfuls to sprinkle on their food.

If you have a conservatory to dine in, or if your dining room is full of natural light, take advantage of this environment to grow herbs in containers (see pages 51–52). Surround the table with pots of delicious-smelling culinary and aromatic herbs. For containers that are intended to be a permanent

Each place setting is adorned with a herbal napkin ring, a finger bowl sprinkled with aromatic herbs and a miniature pot of herbs that acts as a holder for guest name-tags.

feature, choose unusual items such as china basins and chimney pots. Trailing herbs in hanging baskets make romantic decorations; suitable varieties include prostrate rosemary, prostrate sage, creeping thymes, catmint and the colourful nasturtium.

ABOVE LEFT **Float mint and lemon balm in small glass bowls of water to give your visitors a pleasant way to freshen their fingers between courses.**

ABOVE RIGHT **Write the names of your guests on copper plant tags and put them into miniature terracotta plant pots filled with fresh herbs.**

Although they may seem out of place in an office, herbs can do much to enhance your working environment. Particular varieties invigorate and uplift the mind, aiding concentration and inspiration. Keep a pot of fresh herbs on your desk or near your work area, where the leaves and flowers will be lovely to look at and will gently fragrance the air. Essential oils sprinkled onto a tissue or handkerchief are an alternative to fresh herbs and provide a stronger herbal 'hit'. Basil is energizing and invigorating and is used to treat depression. Coriander/cilantro and eucalpytus are also uplifting. Geranium is refreshing and relaxing, as is lavender. Lemon balm bursts with zingy fragrance, and thyme is good for combating depression and fatigue.

Even the paper you use can be scented – either buy it ready-scented or add a few drops of essential oil. Stick dried herbs to paper or leave them loose in a folded letter. A sophisticated flower press is not needed. Simply take a perfect flower or leaf and sandwich it between two piles of blotting or watercolour paper. Put this sandwich between the leaves of a large heavy book and pile three or four more heavy books on top of it. Leave for a couple of weeks, until the herbs have dried out. Ink too can be fragranced. Immerse 25 g/1 oz of dried aromatic flowers (such as myrtle, lavender flowers, lemon verbena, pelargonium or rosemary) in water and bring to the boil. Simmer for 30–40 minutes until it has reduced to 4 teaspoons of pungent dark liquid. Strain, allow to cool and add to a bottle of ordinary ink.

ABOVE **Writing paper can be scented with a few drops of essential oil and decorated with dried pressed herbs. Even the ink you use to write a letter can be fragranced.**

OPPOSITE PAGE **Herbs with colourful and pretty blooms can be dried and pressed in the same way as any wild flowers before being incorporated into eye-catching arrangements.**

RIGHT **As a powerful aid to concentration, place a jugful of fresh herbs such as basil and mint on a desk or elsewhere in a work space.**

Refreshing and invigorating herbs can bring a new sense of purpose to your working space, and revive some of the almost forgotten pleasures of letter writing.

LEFT **This tussie-mussie includes flowering thyme for courage, fennel for strength, lemon balm for sympathy and geranium for comfort.**

RIGHT **A bridal bed decorated with fresh flowering thyme, rosemary, pelargoniums, eucalyptus and roses looks romantic and will fill a room with fresh summer smells.**

Fragrant nosegays and tussie-mussies were traditionally associated with declarations of love or used to ward off dangerous diseases.

Nosegays or tussie-mussies – posies made up of aromatic herbs and flowers – were popular from medieval times not only because of their ability to disguise unlovely smells but also because they were thought to protect the holder from disease. They were also used for declarations of love, since all the flowers and herbs had special meanings. A lover might send a posy of, for example, mint for virtue, forget-me-nots for true love, golden marjoram for blushes, myrtle for love, rosemary for remembrance and ivy for fidelity. Guests will be sure to appreciate such a posy placed on a pillow or at the bedside, even if they have no idea of the signficance of the herbs and flowers used.

To fill a bedroom with summer scent in winter, spray bed linen with a fresh linen spray or sprinkle pillows with a diluted essential oil. Chamomile, lavender, lemon balm and oregano promote sound sleep.

garlanded with scent

To scent a room in winter, when fresh herbs are scarce, you can vaporize an essential herbal oil in a ceramic burner. Add a few drops of oil to water in the bowl and use a nightlight to heat it gently from beneath.

Garlands serve the same purpose as potpourris. They are designed to scent the air and the objects around them, but in a more decorative way. They can be hung on the backs of doors and the corners of beds, or simply placed on a pillow to welcome a guest. Only herbs with tough and pliable stems can be used to make garlands because they must be able to withstand being looped and twisted. For fresh herbal garlands use catmint, lemon balm, lemon verbena, marjorams, mints and scented pelargoniums. Rosemary, lavender, bay, myrtle and eucalpytus are rewarding to use in either fresh or dried form.

An aromatic herbal bath is one of the most pleasurable ways to cleanse your skin and revitalize your whole body. You can add particular herbs to promote relaxation or stimulation.

ABOVE **Put a bar of herbal soap on a bed of fresh mint. An invigorating aroma is released when the leaves are gently crushed.**

ABOVE CENTRE **Fresh herbs can be suspended from the hot tap before the bath is filled with water. Lemon balm and eucalyptus, for example, have a wonderfully revitalizing effect in the morning.**

LEFT AND ABOVE RIGHT **Scatter lavender around the bath and put down a cotton mat to stand on. The scent of crushed herb fills the bathroom and permeates nearby rooms.**

Some herbs invigorate; others soothe the mind and body, promoting peaceful sleep. For stimulation, choose basil, bay, eucalyptus, lemon verbena, mint, rosemary, sage and thyme. For relaxation, the preferred herbs are chamomile, lavender and lemon balm.

To treat minor skin irritations or soothe dry sensitive skin, use calendula, comfrey, fennel, lady's mantle, parsley and spearmint. Any of these herbs can be used, in dried form, in a herbal bath. The herbs should be crushed or ground and put into a muslin/ cheesecloth bag; hang the bag under a hot running tap.

The water in a herbal bath should be close to body temperature; if it is too hot, the skin perspires and fails to take advantage of the therapeutic qualities. To enjoy the full benefits of the bath, wallow in it for at least 10 minutes.

Therapeutic preparations can be made at home from essential oils and herbal infusions.

lavender spritz

For a classic skin freshener, fill an atomizer bottle with distilled water and add a couple of drops of lavender oil. Shake to blend.

lip balm

Oil of eucalyptus, lemon, thyme, jasmine, lavender, geranium, juniper or peppermint

Add 2 drops of the oil of your choice to 1 tablespoon warmed cocoa butter. Scoop into a small screw-top jar and allow to cool.

vinegar bath

Boil leaves of lemon balm and pennyroyal in cider vinegar. Infuse overnight, then strain. Pour into warm water for a refreshing bath.

massage oil

5 drops lavender oil
5 drops neroli oil
6 drops frankincense
50 ml/2 oz almond oil

Add oils to a small stoppered jar and shake to blend. Massage gently into the skin to firm it up and to combat stretch marks.

hand cream

225 ml/scant 1 cup rosewater
60 ml/¼ cup cornflour/cornstarch
60 ml/¼ cup glycerine
3 drops chamomile oil

Blend rosewater, glycerine and cornflour. Heat gently in a double saucepan to thicken, then cool. Stir in oil. Store in screw-top jar.

foot bath

Fresh leaves of bay, eucalyptus, lavender, lemon balm, thyme, marjoram, spearmint

Sprinkle handfuls of herbs into a large bowl. Add 2 teaspoons of salt and enough hot water to cover the feet and ankles. Soak feet for at least 10 minutes while breathing in the delicious aroma.

antiseptic wash

Among oils with antiseptic action are thyme, lavender, tea tree and eucalyptus. Add 8 drops of one of these to a small bowl of water and apply to minor wounds.

rosewater toner

160 ml/scant ¾ cup rosewater
150 ml/scant ⅔ cup witch hazel
6 drops glycerine

Pour all the ingredients into a bottle and shake well before use.

Essential herbal oils or fresh herbs steeped in hot water can be used to create a wide variety of bathroom tonics – or simply to enhance the luxury of bathing.

cooking with herbs

dressings

Dressings such as these do not have to be confined to salads. Use them in marinades, trickle over grilled meat or fish – or pour into a dish and serve as a dip. Combining fresh herbs with the oils and vinegars found in most of these recipes is also a fantastic way of preserving them.

coriander and toasted sesame

This dressing is similar to the traditional Japanese dressing served over wilted spinach. The toasted sesame seeds add a nutty, smoky flavour, which works in beautiful contrast to the freshness of the coriander/cilantro. It is delicious tossed through a mixed noodle and vegetable salad with avocado and tomatoes. If preparing ahead, make sure to give it a really good shake before using.

2 tablespoons sesame seeds
2 large spring onions/scallions, trimmed and chopped
1 tablespoon chopped fresh coriander/cilantro leaves
1 teaspoon caster/superfine sugar
1 tablespoon rice wine vinegar
1 tablespoon light soy sauce
3 tablespoons sunflower oil
2 teaspoons sesame oil
salt and freshly ground black pepper

Makes 150 ml/⅔ cup

Dry fry the sesame seeds in a small frying pan/skillet over a medium heat until toasted and starting to release their aroma. Cool and transfer to a food processor. Blend to a paste with the spring onions/scallions, coriander/cilantro, sugar, vinegar, soy sauce and a pinch of salt. Add the oils and blend again until amalgamated. Adjust seasoning to taste and serve.

dill and orange with walnut oil

The combination of orange, dill and walnut oil is lovely and makes a wonderful dressing for smoked fish salads. You can vary the oil and use hazelnut or extra virgin olive oil, if preferred.

grated zest and juice of 1 orange
1 small shallot, finely chopped
1 small garlic clove, peeled and crushed
1 tablespoon red wine vinegar
4 tablespoons walnut oil
1 tablespoon chopped fresh dill
salt and freshly ground black pepper

Makes 150 ml/⅔ cup

Put the orange zest and juice, shallot, garlic, vinegar and salt and pepper in a bowl and whisk together. Gradually whisk in the oil until the dressing is amalgamated. Stir in the dill to finish. Serve over frisée lettuce leaves with flaked smoked trout, blanched fine green beans and lightly toasted chopped walnuts.

chive and shallot

The flavour of avocado oil is milder than extra virgin olive oil and works really well with the delicate chives and shallot in this dressing. Avocado oil has the most gorgeous deep green luminosity to it, making this a really striking-looking dressing.

1 shallot, very finely chopped
1 tablespoon chopped fresh chives
1 small garlic clove, peeled and crushed
6 tablespoons avocado oil
1 tablespoon lemon juice
a good pinch of caster/superfine sugar
salt and freshly ground black pepper

Makes 125 ml/½ cup

Place all the ingredients in a jar, seal the lid and shake well until the dressing is amalgamated. Adjust seasoning to taste and serve. Serve with a crisp bacon and cos/romaine lettuce salad with garlic croutons.

herbed labne

Labne (labneh or labni) is a thickened yogurt made by straining off the whey and is popular throughout the eastern Mediterranean and Middle East, where it is often served as part of a mezze. The straining process increases the fat content, giving labne a more creamy texture. It is often formed into small balls and stored in oil. It is available to buy from larger supermarkets and specialist food stores (you could use thick Greek yogurt in this recipe instead).

125 g/½ cup labne or thick Greek yogurt
2 tablespoons extra virgin olive oil
1 tablespoon chopped fresh herbs, such
*   as coriander/cilantro, mint and parsley*
2 teaspoons lemon juice
½ teaspoon clear honey
¼ teaspoon smoked paprika
salt and freshly ground black pepper

Makes 200 ml/1 scant cup

Place all the ingredients in a food processor and blend until smooth. Adjust seasoning to taste and serve. Delicious paired with a new potato, chicory, smoked salmon and beetroot/beet salad.

avocado and Tarragon

With its naturally smooth, velvety flesh, avocado is a superb addition to a creamy salad dressing. It works well with lots of herbs but is particularly good with tarragon, and this makes it the perfect dressing for fish- or chicken-based salads – try it as an alternative dressing to a Caesar.

1 small avocado
125 ml/½ cup buttermilk
1 spring onion/scallion, finely chopped
2 tablespoons chopped fresh tarragon
2 tablespoons avocado oil
1½ tablespoons lemon juice
salt and freshly ground black pepper

Makes 300 ml/1¼ cups

Cut the avocado in half and remove the stone. Scoop the flesh into a food processor and add the buttermilk, spring onion/scallion, tarragon, oil, lemon juice and a little salt and pepper and blend until smooth. Thin with milk or water if necessary, adjust seasoning to taste and serve.

greek oregano

The beauty of Greek food is that it contains simple everyday ingredients that are transformed by the sun – big juicy tomatoes and sweet sliced onions topped with brilliant white feta and a scattering of dried rigani, or Greek oregano. In full bloom, the rigani plant reaches almost half a metre (2 feet) in height and has small white flowers. It is cut and dried in long stalks, with the flowers often still attached, and it is universally considered the king of oregano. You can buy packets of rigani in specialist food stores.

6 tablespoons Kalamata olive oil
1 tablespoon red wine vinegar
2 teaspoons rigani or dried oregano
salt and freshly ground black pepper

Makes 75 ml/⅓ cup

Place all the ingredients in a screw top jar and shake well until amalgamated. Allow to rest for 30 minutes for the oregano to soften. Before serving, shake well again. Perfect served with a classic Greek salad of tomatoes, onion, green or black olives and feta.

mint salsa verde

Based on the classic Italian sauce, this dressing is thinned a little with boiling water to give a pouring consistency suitable to dress salads. It is best used straight away while the mint remains a bright green colour, but if you want to make it ahead of time, omit the lemon juice until just before serving.

½ bunch of fresh mint leaves, roughly chopped
1 garlic clove, peeled and crushed
1 tablespoon drained capers
2 pitted green olives, chopped
2 teaspoons lemon juice
½ teaspoon caster/superfine sugar
5 tablespoons extra virgin olive oil
1 tablespoon boiling water
salt and freshly ground black pepper

Makes 125 ml/½ cup

Put the mint leaves, garlic, capers, olives, lemon juice, sugar, salt and pepper in a food processor and blend until as finely chopped as possible. Add the oil and water and blend again until you have an evenly blended, vibrant green dressing. Adjust seasoning to taste.

This is fabulous poured over a char-grilled lamb salad with haricot beans, steamed potatoes and rocket/arugula leaves.

mexican lime, coriander and chipotle chilli

Chipotle chillies/chiles have a wonderfully smoky flavour and aroma, giving this dressing a beautiful rich quality. You can buy dried chipotle chillies/chiles if you prefer but the paste, available from specialist food stores, is perfect for dressings. Both agave syrup and pumpkin seed oil will be available in health food stores.

1–2 teaspoons dried chipotle chilli/chile paste
grated zest and juice of 1 lime
1 teaspoon agave syrup
3 tablespoons pumpkin seed oil or avocado oil
1 tablespoon chopped fresh coriander/cilantro
salt and freshly ground black pepper

Makes 75 ml/⅓ cup

Combine the chilli/chile paste, lime zest and juice, agave syrup and a little salt and pepper in a bowl and whisk until smooth. Gradually whisk in the oil until smooth, stir in the coriander/cilantro and serve.

Try drizzling this dressing over a shredded chicken, corn and avocado salad on a warm tortilla.

sauces

Herb-based sauces or spreads are extremely versatile and can be served as dips for crudités, stirred through pasta or spooned onto grilled fish or poultry. Herb butters add a lovely finishing touch to cooked meat or vegetables and are easy to make. Simply beat your favourite herb into some softened butter, perhaps adding a little pepper or lemon juice. Wrap in clingfilm/plastic wrap and chill until required.

pesto

Over the past 20 years, this thick, aromatic herb and nut sauce from Genoa has travelled widely and is now used by cooks throughout the world to serve with pasta or grilled fish, or be stirred into vegetable soup. Once made, cover the surface with a little extra olive oil, seal in a container and refrigerate for up to 5 days.

2 handfuls of fresh basil leaves
1 garlic clove, peeled and crushed
2 tablespoons pine nuts
a pinch of sea salt
6–8 tablespoons extra virgin olive oil
2 tablespoons freshly grated Parmesan cheese
freshly ground black pepper

Makes 150 ml/⅔ cup

Put the basil, garlic, pine nuts and sea salt in a mortar and pound to form a fairly smooth paste. Add the olive oil slowly until you reach a texture that is soft but not runny. Add the Parmesan and pepper to taste. Cover the surface with a little olive oil and refrigerate for up to 5 days.

tip You can make this sauce in a food processor, but do not over-process otherwise the sauce will become too smooth.

foaming sage butter

This is so simple, yet totally delicious – melted butter is sautéed until golden and nutty then mixed with fresh sage leaves and a little crushed garlic. It is particularly good with pumpkin ravioli, spinach and ricotta gnocchi, seared swordfish, or simply with plain noodles.

Melt the butter in a small frying pan/skillet until it stops foaming, then cook over medium heat for 3–4 minutes until it turns golden brown. Remove the pan from the heat and add the sage leaves, garlic, and a little seasoning. Leave to sizzle in the butter for 30 seconds until fragrant.

125 g/1 stick unsalted butter
2 tablespoons chopped fresh sage
2 garlic cloves, peeled and crushed
sea salt and freshly ground black pepper

Serves 2

parsley sauce

A modern adaptation of parsley sauce, traditionally made using a roux base. This lighter version is wonderful with a poached salmon fillet, or steamed or baked white fish.

3½ tablespoons unsalted butter
175 ml/⅔ cup whipping cream
a handful of fresh flat leaf parsley leaves
sea salt and freshly ground white pepper

Serves 4

Heat the butter and cream together in a saucepan until the butter has melted, then boil for 1 minute. Transfer to a food processor with the parsley leaves and blend until very smooth and green. Season to taste. Heat through and serve hot.

agro dolce sauce

This sauce is typical of many from southern Sicily, where sultanas/golden raisins and capers are added to a tomato base to produce a lovely sweet and savoury flavour. It is great served with grilled swordfish or oily fish such as tuna or mackerel.

3 tablespoons extra virgin olive oil
2 garlic cloves, peeled and finely chopped
grated zest of 1 unwaxed lemon
a pinch of dried chilli flakes/hot pepper flakes
500 g/2 lb. ripe tomatoes, peeled and chopped
2 anchovy fillets in oil, drained and chopped
2 tablespoons capers in brine, drained

50 g/⅓ cup sultanas/golden raisins
2 teaspoons red wine vinegar
1 teaspoon caster/superfine sugar
2 tablespoons pine nuts, toasted
1 tablespoon chopped fresh flat leaf parsley
sea salt and freshly ground black pepper

Serves 4

Heat the olive oil in a saucepan and gently fry the garlic, lemon zest and chilli flakes/hot pepper flakes with a little seasoning for 2–3 minutes, or until soft but not browned. Add the tomatoes, anchovies, capers, sultanas/golden raisins, vinegar and sugar and heat gently, partially covered, for 3–4 minutes, or until the tomatoes have softened. Stir in the pine nuts and parsley and season to taste. Serve hot.

light dishes

summer leaf and herb salad

There are thousands of recipes for simple leaf salads, incorporating a delicious mixture of fresh herbs ensures a version that will always impress.

inner leaves from 2 large cos/romaine lettuces
250 g/8 oz. mixed salad leaves, such as radicchio, mâche (lamb's lettuce or corn salad), mizuna or chicory/endive
a handful of mixed, fresh soft-leaf herbs such as basil, chives, dill and mint

Dressing
1 garlic clove, peeled and crushed
125 ml/½ cup extra virgin olive oil
1 tablespoon lemon juice
1 teaspoon clear honey
1 teaspoon Dijon mustard
sea salt and freshly ground black pepper

Serves 4

Put the dressing ingredients into a bowl or small jug/pitcher and set aside to infuse for at least 1 hour. Just before serving, strain out the garlic. Wash the leaves, spin dry in a salad spinner (or pat dry with paper towels) and transfer to a plastic bag. Chill for 30 minutes to make the leaves crisp. Put the leaves and herbs into a large bowl, add a little of the dressing and toss well to coat evenly. Add a little more dressing to taste, then serve.

homemade herb cheese

Making soft cheese from scratch is surprisingly easy and very satisfying. Adapt the basic recipe and experiment with different combinations of herbs to create your own bespoke cheese.

500 g/1¾ cups thick yogurt or 400 g/1⅔ cups plain yogurt
100 g/¼ cup double cream/heavy cream
1 garlic clove, peeled and crushed
3 tablespoons chopped fresh basil
3 tablespoons chopped mixed fresh herbs,
*   including dill, marjoram, parsley and thyme leaves*
sea salt and freshly ground black pepper
wholemeal/whole wheat or soda bread, to serve
a piece of muslin/cheesecloth, 30 cm/12 in. square

Serves 4–6

Put all the ingredients into a bowl and stir well. Line a second bowl with a large piece of muslin/cheesecloth and spoon in the yogurt mixture. Pull up the ends of the muslin/cheesecloth to form a bag and tie tightly with string.

Hang the bag over the bowl so the liquid can drain from the yogurt. Leave in a cool place overnight. Unwrap the bag and transfer the cheese to a serving bowl. Serve with lightly toasted wholemeal/whole wheat or soda bread.

smoked duck rice paper rolls

Fresh spring rolls, often called 'summer rolls' are perfect carriers for a variety of herbs. Due to their refreshing nature, they are typically served in summer months and can have many different fillings. This recipe uses Thai basil leaves and smoked duck breast (available from specialist food stores), which adds a further intriguing flavour to these delicious rolls.

100 g/3½ oz. rice vermicelli noodles
2 teaspoons fish sauce
2 teaspoons freshly squeezed lime juice
2 teaspoons caster/granulated sugar
8 x 20-cm/8-in. dried rice paper wrappers
100 g/3½ oz. smoked duck breast (see tip)
100 g/3 cups thinly sliced lettuce
1 carrot, peeled and cut into thin batons
½ cucumber, deseeded and cut into batons
20 fresh Thai basil leaves

Dipping sauce
2 tablespoons hoisin sauce
1 tablespoon smooth peanut butter
1 tablespoon warm water
2 teaspoons freshly squeezed lime juice
1 teaspoon dark soy sauce
¼ teaspoon caster/granulated sugar

Serves 4

Put the noodles in a bowl, cover with boiling water and soak for 30 minutes until softened. Drain the noodles, pat dry and transfer to a large mixing bowl. Whisk the fish sauce, lime juice and sugar together until the sugar is dissolved and pour over the noodles. Toss well and set aside.

Next make the dipping sauce. Put all the ingredients in a small saucepan set over a low heat. Heat gently, stirring until the peanut butter is softened and the sauce smooth. Remove from the heat and set aside to cool.

Working one at a time, dip the rice paper wrappers into a bowl of warm water for about a minute until softened and then pat dry on paper towels. Lay each wrapper out flat and top with a few noodles, the smoked duck slices, shredded lettuce, carrot, cucumber and basil leaves. Fold the ends of the rice paper over the filling and then roll up tightly to form parcels. Serve with the dipping sauce.

Tip If you can't find smoked duck you could use smoked salmon or smoked trout instead.

mee grob

Sometimes called 'mee krob', this crispy noodle dish is a delicious and fragrant Thai appetizer. Be careful when deep-frying noodles as the oil bubbles up quite dramatically. Yellow bean sauce is available from most large supermarkets or specialist stores, but hoisin can be used instead.

100 g/3½ oz. dried rice vermicelli noodles
2 eggs, beaten
125 g/1 cup firm tofu, cubed
1 tablespoon dried shrimp
1 Asian shallot, thinly sliced
1 tablespoon pickled garlic
50 g/1 cup beansprouts, trimmed
a small bunch of fresh coriander/cilantro
6 garlic chives, roughly chopped
vegetable oil, for deep-frying

Sauce
125 g/½ cup plus 1 tablespoon grated
  palm sugar
1 tablespoon yellow bean sauce
2 tablespoons fish sauce
1 tablespoon freshly squeezed lime juice

Serves 4

Put the noodles in a bowl, cover with boiling water and soak for 20 minutes until softened. Drain the noodles and pat dry with paper towels.

Next make the sauce. Put the palm sugar in a saucepan with 1 tablespoon cold water set over a low heat. Heat gently, stirring continuously, until the sugar dissolves. Turn up the heat and boil for a minute until the syrup turns lightly golden, then stir in the yellow bean paste, fish sauce and lime juice. Simmer gently for 3–4 minutes until thick and keep warm until ready to use.

Pour vegetable oil into a wok or large saucepan to reach about 5 cm/2 in. up the side and set over a medium–high heat. Heat until a cube of bread dropped into the oil crisps in 30 seconds. Add the noodles in small bunches and fry for 1–2 minutes until crisp and golden. Remove with a slotted spoon and drain on paper towels. Repeat with the remaining noodles until you have fried them all. Keep the pan on the heat.

Break the noodles into a large mixing bowl and set aside.

Strain the beaten egg through a fine mesh sieve/strainer and pour half into the hot oil – it will puff up into a lacy cake. Fry for 30 seconds, flip over and fry for a further 30 seconds until crisp and brown, then remove with a slotted spoon. Drain on paper towels and repeat with the remaining egg.

Deep-fry the tofu and set aside. Deep-fry the dried shrimp for 10 seconds and remove with a slotted spoon. Carefully discard all but 1 tablespoon of the oil and stir-fry the shallot and garlic for 5 minutes until lightly crisp. Stir in the beansprouts and remove the pan from the heat. Add all the fried ingredients along with the coriander/cilantro and garlic chives to the noodles and stir to combine. Pour in the sauce, stir again and serve at once.

barbecued fish bathed in oregano and lemon

This dish of char-grilled bream with oil, oregano and garlic, is just perfect for an al fresco lunch, but you could use other small fish such as red mullet, snapper or even trout.

2 unwaxed lemons
250 ml/1 cup extra virgin olive oil
1 tablespoon dried oregano
2 garlic cloves, peeled and finely chopped
2 tablespoons chopped fresh flat leaf parsley

6 snapper or bream, about 350 g/12 oz. each,
  well cleaned and scaled
sea salt and freshly ground black pepper

Serves 6

Grate the zest of 1 lemon into a small bowl and squeeze in the juice. Add 225 ml/¾ cup of the oil, the oregano, garlic, parsley, salt and pepper. Leave to infuse for at least 1 hour.

Wash and dry the fish inside and out. Using a sharp knife, cut several slashes into each side. Squeeze the juice from the remaining lemon into a bowl, add the remaining 4 tablespoons of oil, salt and pepper and rub the mixture all over the fish.

Heat the flat plate of your barbecue for 10 minutes, add the fish and cook for 3–4 minutes on each side until charred and cooked through. Alternatively, use a large, heavy-based frying pan/skillet or stove-top grill pan. Transfer to a large, warm platter, pour over the dressing and let rest for 5 minutes before serving.

souvlaki with cracked wheat and herb salad

Souvlaki is the classic Greek kebab/kabob, a delicious combination of cubed lamb marinated in red wine with herbs and lemon juice.

1 kg/2 lb. neck end of lamb
1 tablespoon chopped fresh rosemary
1 tablespoon dried oregano
1 onion, chopped
4 garlic cloves, peeled and chopped
300 ml/1¼ cups red wine
juice of 1 lemon
75 ml/⅓ cup olive oil
sea salt and freshly ground black pepper

Salad
350 g/3¼ cups cracked wheat (bulghur wheat)
2 handfuls of chopped fresh parsley
a handful of chopped fresh mint leaves
2 garlic cloves, peeled and crushed
150 ml/½ cup extra virgin olive oil
juice of 2 lemons
a pinch of caster/superfine sugar
sea salt and freshly ground black pepper
6 large rosemary stalks or metal skewers

Serves 6

Trim any large pieces of fat from the lamb and then cut the meat into 2.5 cm/1 in. cubes. Put into a shallow, non-metal dish. Add the rosemary, oregano, onion, garlic, wine, lemon juice, olive oil, salt and pepper. Toss well, cover and let marinate in the refrigerator for 4 hours. Return to room temperature for 1 hour before cooking.

To make the salad, soak the cracked wheat in warm water for 30 minutes until the water has been absorbed and the grains have softened. Strain well to extract any excess water and transfer the wheat to a bowl. Add all the remaining ingredients, season to taste and set aside for 30 minutes to develop the flavours.

Thread the lamb onto large rosemary stalks or metal skewers. Cook on a preheated barbecue or under a grill/broiler for 10 minutes, turning and basting from time to time. Let rest for 5 minutes, then serve with the salad.

main meals

spaghetti bolognese

The addition of chicken livers along with fresh bay leaves and thyme brings a great depth of flavour to this Italian classic. Other than pairing with spaghetti, you can use the sauce as the base for lasagne or other baked pasta dishes.

125 g/4 oz. smoked pancetta, diced
2 tablespoons extra virgin olive oil
1 large onion, finely chopped
2 garlic cloves, peeled and finely chopped
1 tablespoon chopped fresh thyme
750 g/1½ lb. minced/ground beef
50 g/2 oz chicken livers, diced
300 ml/1¼ cups red wine
two 400-g/14-oz. cans chopped tomatoes
2 tablespoons tomato purée/tomato paste
a pinch of caster/granulated sugar
2 fresh bay leaves
sea salt and freshly ground black pepper
500 g/1 lb. 2 oz. dry spaghetti

Serves 4–6

Heat a saucepan and dry-fry the pancetta for 3–4 minutes, or until browned and the fat is released into the pan. Remove from the pan with a slotted spoon. Add the olive oil to the pan and gently fry the onion, garlic and thyme for 10 minutes, or until softened. Increase the heat, add the minced/ground beef and livers and stir-fry for 5 minutes, or until browned.

Add the wine and bring to the boil, then stir in the canned tomatoes, tomato purée/tomato paste, sugar, bay leaves and seasoning. Cover and simmer over low heat for 1–1½ hours, or until the sauce has thickened.

Cook and drain the spaghetti according to the packet instructions. Discard the bay leaves from the sauce, season to taste and serve with the pasta.

pasta with melted ricotta and herby parmesan sauce

This pasta dish is fast and fresh, with the ricotta melting into the hot pasta and coating it like a creamy sauce. The pine nuts give it crunch, while the herbs lend a fresh, scented flavour. If you don't have all the herbs listed here, use just rocket/arugula plus one other – the parsley or basil suggested, or perhaps chives, snipped with scissors/shears.

350 g/12 oz. dried penne or other pasta
6 tablespoons extra virgin olive oil
100 g/1 cup pine nuts
125 g/4 oz. rocket/arugula leaves, chopped
2 tablespoons chopped fresh flat leaf parsley
2 tablespoons chopped fresh basil
250 g/1 cup fresh ricotta cheese, mashed
50 g/½ cup freshly grated Parmesan cheese
sea salt and freshly ground black pepper

Serves 4

Cook the pasta according to the instructions on the packet. Meanwhile, heat the olive oil in a frying pan/skillet, add the pine nuts and fry gently until golden. Set aside.

Drain the cooked pasta, reserving 4 tablespoons of the cooking liquid, and return both to the pan. Add the pine nuts and their olive oil, the herbs, ricotta, half the Parmesan and plenty of ground black pepper. Stir until evenly coated. Serve in warmed bowls, with the remaining cheese sprinkled on top.

paella with artichokes and broad beans

A refreshing version of a Spanish classic in which the flavour of mint complements the vegetables perfectly. You really do need to use fresh artichokes here, they can be seen growing everywhere along the coastal regions of Spain in the summer, so it is hardly surprising to find a dish dedicated to this striking vegetable.

4 medium artichokes, halved or quartered
1 lemon, halved
4 tablespoons extra virgin olive oil
2 bay leaves, bruised
4 garlic cloves, peeled and crushed
1 onion, finely chopped
1.2 litres/5 cups hot vegetable stock
250 g/2 cups shelled and peeled
   broad/fava beans

350 g/scant 2 cups bomba, Calasparra
   or arborio rice
2 tablespoons chopped fresh mint
sea salt and freshly ground black pepper
alioli, to serve

Serves 4

Start by preparing the artichokes. Cut the stems off to about 2 cm/¾ in. and the leaves down to about 3–4 cm/1¼–1½ in. from the top. Peel away and discard any tough leaves to reveal the round base. In the centre there will be a hairy 'choke'. Scoop this out and discard it. Cut the bases in half and put them into a bowl filled with cold water. Squeeze in the juice from both lemon halves, and put the squeezed halves in the water too.

Heat the oil in a 35-cm/14-in. paella pan (or shallow flameproof casserole) and add the bay leaves. Fry gently for about 30 seconds, until fragrant, and then stir in the garlic, onion and a little salt and pepper. Lower the heat and cook for 20 minutes, until the onion is caramelized. Add the artichoke halves and stock, bring to the boil and simmer gently for 10 minutes.

Stir in the broad/fava beans, rice and mint, and simmer gently for 20 minutes, until the rice is al dente and the liquid absorbed. Let sit for 10 minutes before serving with a bowl of alioli.

spinach, rice and bean soup

The addition of rosemary makes this wintery soup extra delicious. Serve with chargrilled sourdough rubbed with a clove of garlic for an indulgent main meal.

2 tablespoons extra virgin olive oil, plus
*   extra to serve*
125 g/4½ oz. diced pancetta or bacon
1 onion, finely chopped
2 garlic cloves, peeled and crushed
1 tablespoon chopped fresh rosemary
grated zest and freshly squeezed juice
*   of ½ unwaxed lemon*
150 g/generous ¾ cup bomba, Calasparra or
*   arborio rice*
400-g/14-oz. can haricot/navy beans, drained
1.5 litres/generous 6 cups hot chicken stock

350 g/ ¾ lb. spinach
sea salt and freshly ground black pepper
6 slices toasted sourdough bread rubbed
*   with a peeled clove of garlic, to serve*

Serves 6

Heat the oil in a large saucepan and fry the pancetta for 5 minutes, until golden.

Add the onion, garlic, rosemary and lemon zest to the pan with a little salt and pepper, and fry gently for 5 minutes, until the onion is softened. Stir in the rice and beans, and add the stock. Bring to the boil and simmer gently for 15 minutes.

Meanwhile wash and dry the spinach leaves, discarding any thick stalks. Shred the leaves. Stir the spinach into the soup with the lemon juice and cook for a further 5 minutes until the rice is cooked and the spinach wilted.

Season the soup to taste, drizzle over a little olive oil and serve immediately with the garlic-rubbed toasted sourdough.

beef pho

It's the large baskets of colourful herbs and condiments that give this classic soup its freshness and that unique flavour and texture. To allow the flavours to develop, you need to prepare this dish a day in advance.

1 kg/2 lb. beef short ribs
5 cm/2 in. fresh ginger, peeled,
  sliced and pounded
1 onion, sliced
2 garlic cloves, peeled and sliced
3 whole star anise, pounded
2 cinnamon sticks, pounded
400 g/14 oz. dried rice stick noodles
350 g/1⅓ cups thinly sliced beef fillet
3 tablespoons fish sauce
1 teaspoon salt
1 teaspoon caster/granulated sugar
freshly squeezed juice of 1 lime
125 g/2⅓ cups beansprouts, trimmed

Garnishes
2 red bird's eye chillies/chiles, chopped
a handful each of fresh Thai basil,
  Vietnamese mint and coriander/cilantro
6 spring onions/scallions, trimmed
  and sliced

Serves 4

Put the ribs in a large saucepan, cover with cold water and bring to the boil. Simmer for 10 minutes then drain and wash the ribs. Return them to the pan and add 2 litres/3½ cups more cold water along with the ginger, onion, garlic, star anise and cinnamon. Return to the boil and simmer gently for 1½ hours, or until the meat is tender.

Carefully remove the ribs from the stock and set aside to cool. Thinly shred the meat, discarding the bones. Strain the stock through a fine mesh sieve/strainer and set aside to cool. Refrigerate both the meat and the stock overnight.

The next day, soak the noodles in a bowlful of hot water for 20–30 minutes, until softened. Drain well, shake dry and divide the noodles between large bowls.

Meanwhile, skim and discard the layer of fat from the cold stock and return the pan to a medium heat until just boiling. Stir in the shredded meat, beef fillet, fish sauce, salt, sugar and lime juice. Place the beef fillet on the noodles, spoon over the stock and top with the beansprouts.

Serve with a plate of the garnishes in the middle of the table for everyone to help themselves.

drinks and sweet things

jasmine and lychee iced tea

There are rather exotic flavors in this iced tea – if you are lucky enough to find fresh lychees you can use those and simply add a little honey for sweetness, otherwise canned lychees in a light syrup are fine. The flavour of mint goes well with most iced teas; the leaves also make a pretty garnish.

1 tablespoon jasmine tea leaves
1 litre/quart just-boiled water
2 star anise, bashed lightly
400-g/14-oz. can lychees in syrup
lime wedges, to serve
fresh mint leaves, to garnish
sparkling lemonade/lemon soda, to top up
ice cubes, to serve

Serves 6

Put the tea leaves in a warmed teapot or heatproof jug/pitcher and pour in the just-boiled water. Leave to infuse for 5 minutes then strain the tea into a clean jug/pitcher. Add the star anise and let cool.

Half-fill 6 tall glasses with ice and chilled tea. Add 3 lychees and 2 tablespoons of the syrup to each one. Finish with a few lime wedges and mint sprigs in each glass and top up with lemonade/lemon soda to serve.

gingerella punch

This sophisticated summer punch combines the flavours of melon, ginger and basil – it makes for an ideal drink to share with friends on a balmy evening.

750 g/1½ lb. mixed melon flesh, such as watermelon, honeydew and galia, diced
750-ml bottle/6 cups ginger wine, such as Stone's or Crabbie's
dry ginger ale, to top up
a handful of small fresh basil leaves, to garnish
ice cubes, to serve

Serves 12

Put the melon and ginger wine in a large jug/pitcher and chill for 1 hour.

When ready to serve, transfer to a punch bowl and add a few scoops of ice, pour in the ginger ale to taste and add the basil leaves. Ladle into tumblers or wine goblets to serve, spooning a little melon into each, if liked.

salad in a glass

A vegetable cocktail is a great source of vitamins, minerals and antioxidants. The parsley in this recipe will add to the goodness as well as the fresh flavour.

2 small oranges
200 g/7 oz. cos/romaine or butter lettuce
1 green (bell) pepper, cored and deseeded
2 green apples
125 g/4 oz. cucumber
½ bunch of parsley leaves

Serves 3

Peel the oranges and cut the flesh into smallish chunks. Cut the lettuce, (bell) pepper, apples and cucumber into pieces small enough to fit through the funnel on your juicer. Press all the ingredients through the juicer into a jug/pitcher.

warm chocolate and mint cream

This is a sumptuous drink for a chilly winter's evening – sweet and chocolatey with a wonderful mint flavour. You can add more or less mint sprigs to taste.

500 ml/2 cups organic milk
4 sprigs of mint
100 g/3½ oz dark/bittersweet chocolate, finely chopped
1 teaspoon caster sugar
75 ml/½ cup whipped cream

Serves 2

Put the milk and mint sprigs in a saucepan and bring to the boil over low heat. As soon as the milk boils, remove the pan from the heat and let infuse for 15 minutes.

Discard the mint sprigs and reheat the milk to boiling point. Remove the pan from the heat and stir in the chocolate and sugar until melted. Transfer to a food processor and blend until frothy. Pour into 2 mugs and spoon over the whipped cream.

lemon, thyme and green tea sorbet

You can experiment with different flavours with this delightfully elegant herby sorbet, based on the recipe for tea sorbet in Caroline Liddell and Robin Weir's definitive book 'Ices'. Try Earl Grey tea with lemon balm or jasmine tea with lemon and ginger.

3 green tea teabags
200 g/1 cup caster/superfine sugar
1 tablespoon thyme sprigs, preferably lemon thyme
thinly pared zest of 2 lemons
freshly squeezed juice of up to 1½ lemons
1 egg white, lightly beaten (optional)

Serves 6–8

Place the teabags in a bowl and pour over 500 ml/ 2 cups cold water, cover and leave overnight. The next day, dissolve the sugar in 250 ml/1 cup water in a saucepan over low heat and bring to the boil. Take off the heat and pour into a heatproof bowl, then add the thyme and lemon zest. Let the syrup cool, cover, then chill in the refrigerator overnight.

The next day, strain both mixtures into a bowl or jug/pitcher and stir in lemon juice to taste. Chill, then churn in an ice cream maker according to the manufacturer's instructions, and then freeze.

If making by hand, turn into a freezerproof container to make a shallow layer and freeze until hard around the edges. Turn into a food processor, add the egg white and process until smooth. Repeat the freezing and beating once more, then allow to freeze firm. To serve, let the sorbet soften in the refrigerator for 15–20 minutes.

a-z of herbs

A selection of herbs that flavour food or provide garden ornament.
(Heights given are the maximum heights to which plants can grow in optimum conditions.)

Agastache foeniculum
Anise hyssop

Aromatic, hardy, short-lived perennial that grows to 60 cm (2 ft) in flower. Heart-shaped leaves with scalloped edges. Purple or whitish flower spikes in summer. Sow seed in pots in heated propagator in spring. Grows in full sun in average soil, but does best in moist loam. Add dried flower spikes and leaves to potpourri.

Allium fistulosum
Welsh onion

Hardy evergreen perennial, also known as Japanese onion or Japanese leek. Flowers from second year, and reaches 60–90 cm (2–3 ft). Growth similar to spring onion/scallion, but has larger stems. Overwinters in coldest conditions. Sow in fertile soil in sun in spring, or divide clumps. Harvest whole onions, or chop leaves as you would chives.

Allium sativum
Garlic

Hardy perennial grown as an annual. Reaches 40–60 cm (16–24 in). Narrow leaves similar to those of leeks. Plant in autumn in full sun; harvest as soon as leaves die down. Bulbs are delicious roasted; also used in marinades and salad dressings and to flavour meat. Wild garlic (A. ursinum) needs moist woodland conditions; leaves are added to salads and soups.

Allium schoenoprasum
Chives

Hardy perennial with fine green foliage and mauve or white pompom flowers. Depending on species or variety, grows to 30–40 cm (12–16 in) with a spread of 10–20 cm (4–8 in). Grow in full sun in moisture-retentive soil; divide congested clumps in spring or autumn. Flowers and leaves are used in salads, egg dishes and soups. Add to hot dishes at the last moment to prevent loss of flavour.

Allium tuberosum
Chinese chives, garlic chives

Hardy perennial that grows to 30 cm (12 in). Leaves are as long as ordinary chives but flattened and have a strong garlic aroma. Sow seed outside in late spring; divide clumps in spring. Good in salads and cooked dishes.

Aloe barbadensis
Aloe vera

Succulent half-hardy perennial with fleshy spike-edged leaves. Can grow to 60 cm (2 ft) in a large pot, but is usually much smaller. Sow seed in pots in propagator at 21°C (70°F); germination is erratic – do not lose hope if nothing happens in the first year. Propagate from offshoots in summer. Use loam-based compost with added grit. Water sparingly and repot in spring. Plants can be grown outside in summer but must be overwintered in a frost-free place, at a minimum of 5°C (40°F). The gel from its leaf soothes minor burns and cuts; also used in cosmetic preparations.

Aloysia triphylla
syn. *Lippia citriodora*
Lemon verbena

Half-hardy deciduous perennial. Grows to 3 m (10 ft) with a spread of 2.5 m (8 ft). Pale-green and lemon-scented lance-shaped leaves; terminal panicles of lilac-tinged white flowers. Likes full sun and free-draining light soil. If grown in garden against a sunny wall, needs frost protection. A good deep mulch will keep plant safe in milder climates; in colder areas pot it up and overwinter in frost-free greenhouse. Grow from seed or softwood cuttings in spring. Take cuttings from ripened wood in late summer. A relaxing tisane can be made from the leaves; also used to scent vinegars; dried, it is added to potpourri or herb pillows.

Anethum graveolens
Dill

Annual varying in height from 60 cm (2 ft) to 150 cm (5 ft). Some varieties are suited to leaf or seed production. Dill needs well-drained gritty soil and full sun. Sow seed in rows as soon as soil warms up in spring. Thin to about 20 cm (8 in) apart to make sturdy plants. Water in the mornings; plants will run to seed if kept too dry. Sow in succession for a good kitchen supply.

Angelica archangelica
Angelica

Biennial or short-lived perennial that dies after flowering. Grows up to 2.5 m (8 ft), but usually 1–1.5 m (3–5 ft). A good ornamental plant in a herb border in part-shade. Self-seeds copiously. Cooking angelica with rhubarb reduces the need for added sugar; stems can be candied. Should be used medicinally only on medical advice and never by diabetes sufferers.

Anthriscus cerefolium
Chervil

Hardy annual that reaches 30–60 cm (1–2 ft) in flower. Sow seed in light soil. Part shade is best for production of abundant leaves. In a hot dry climate goes to seed prematurely. A component of the traditional *fines herbes* bundle.

Armoracia rusticana
Horseradish

Hardy perennial. Grows to 60–90 cm (24–36 in). A. rusticana 'Variegata' has prettily marked leaves in cream and green and makes a fine centrepiece in a herb garden (though the flavour is not as good or strong for culinary use as that of the non-variegated type).

Cichorium intybus Chicory   *Coriandrum sativum* Coriander/cilantro   *Helichrysum italicum* Curry plant

Artemisia dracunculus
Tarragon
French tarragon grows to 90 cm (3 ft);
Russian tarragon, *A. dracunculoides*, is
slightly taller, reaching 1.2 m (4 ft). Both
have a spread of 45 cm (18 in). Grow in
a dry sunny site with winter protection.
Propagate French tarragon from root
cuttings; it is not as hardy as the Russian
variety and has no viable seed. Tarragon
is good with chicken and fish; French
tarragon has much the better flavour.

Atriplex hortensis
Orach
Annual grown as a culinary and an
ornamental herb. Grows to 1.5 m (4 ft) or
more, with a spread of 30 cm (12 in); can
grow higher, depending on the quality of
the soil. Seed heads are used in cut-flower
arrangements in some countries. Use
tender young leaves in cooking: a popular
spinach substitute in Europe.

Barbarea verna
Landcress
Hardy biennial that grows to 20–70 cm
(8–28 in) with a spread of 20 cm (8 in).
Sow in rich moist soil, in summer for
winter use and in spring for summer use.
Prefers sun but will grow in all but
deepest shade. Peppery flavour of leaves
makes them a good watercress substitute
in salads; use before plant flowers.

Borago officinalis
Borage
Hardy annual that grows to about 60 cm
(24 in); sometimes plants overwinter and
grow into a second season. Bristly
branches, and leaves with a strong

cucumber-like smell; blue or white star-like
flowers. Sow seed in spring. Grow in light
soil in a sunny position. Edible flowers can
be crystallized for decorative use or added
fresh to fruit cups. Borage may cause
contact dermatitis.

Buxus sempervirens
Box
Hardy to half-hardy evergreen used
extensively as an edging plant in herb
gardens. Grows from 1 m (3 ft) to 5 m
(15 ft), and higher in old unclipped
specimens. Leaves are neatly egg-shaped
to elliptical, often glossy dark to mid-
green, and some cultivars are variegated.
Box grows in sun or shade; prefers
alkaline soil but, as long as the ground is
not waterlogged, is not too fussy. If a
hedge is planted, prepare the soil well
with compost and well-rotted manure.
Take cuttings in spring or summer. Box
has no culinary use and all parts are
poisonous. It has traditional medical uses.

Calendula officinalis
Pot marigold
Hardy annual, but some plants will
overwinter successfully. Grows to 60 cm
(24 in). Daisy-like flowers, single or
double, vary in colour from pale cream to
deep orange. Whole plant is aromatic.
Marigold grows in most soils in full sun.
Sow seed in spring or autumn. Self-sown
seedlings are capable of overwintering in
sheltered outside positions, but don't rely
on this. Deadhead plants regularly to
extend flowering season. Culinary and
medicinal plant; also used in cosmetic
preparations. Dried petals look good in
potpourri.

Chamaemelum nobile
Chamomile
Height varies from 6 cm (2.5 in) to 60 cm
(24 in) depending on species or cultivar.
Non-flowering 'Treneague' – the
chamomile commonly used for
chamomile lawns – is increased by
division and the taking of cuttings, as
is the double-flowered chamomile. For
others, sow seed in pots or straight into
the ground; use bottom heat for pots in
spring and sow in ground when it has
warmed up. Grow in free-draining soil
in full sun. Main uses are cosmetic and
medicinal.

Chenopodium bonus-henricus
Good King Henry
Perennial that can reach 60 cm (24 in)
with a spread of 45 cm (18 in). Sow seed
in fertile soil in spring in a sunny position.
Thin out to 25 cm (10 in) apart. Leaves
used as a spinach substitute. Seeds are
mildly laxative; do not use if you suffer
from kidney problems or rheumatism.

Cichorium intybus
Chicory
Hardy perennial reaching a height in
flower of 1 m (3 ft). Leaves are long,
blunt and spear-shaped, with coarsely
toothed edges. Blue flowers from
summer to autumn. Sow seed in spring
in open sunny situation; prefers alkaline
soil but will grow almost anywhere.
Leaves are added to salads.

Coriandrum sativum
Coriander/cilantro
Tender annual growing to 60–70 cm (24–28 in) with a spread of about 30 cm (12 in). *C. sativum.* 'Cilantro' is best for leaf production and *C. sativum.* 'Morocco' for seed. Sow seed in spring in a light well-drained soil when threat of frost is past and soil has warmed. Thin seedlings as they grow and water for leaf production, but do not overwater. Seeds and leaves are used in cooking and medicinally.

Cryptotaenia japonica
Japanese parsley, mitsuba
Hardy perennial that grows to 30 cm (12 in) before flowering and 60–90 cm (2–3 ft) in flower. Leaf is like celery; white flowers dotted about in small umbels. Likes moist conditions in part shade. Grows in sun or in the shade of larger plants in moisture-retentive soil. Leaves and stems used in cooking.

Curcuma longa
Turmeric
Perennial tropical herb of the ginger family. Can be grown as a container plant in temperate climates, but needs winter protection. Grow in a peat and loam mixture, with added grit or sharp sand. Likes warm moist air conditions. Do not overwater. Root is dried and ground into powder for culinary and medicinal uses.

Cymbopogon citratus
Lemon grass
Perennial tropical grass with a strong lemon scent that reaches 60–90 cm (2–3 ft) in the greenhouse. Grow in pots from offshoots or seed. Use peat and loam mixture, with added grit or sharp sand to ensure good drainage. Do not overwater. Likes consistently warm conditions; reduce watering or do not water at all if it is overcast or raining for any length of time. Used in Indian and Thai cookery.

Dianthus species
Pinks
Height varies from 15 cm (8 in) to 60 cm (24 in), depending on species. Grow from softwood cuttings in spring or heel cuttings in late summer. Some older cultivars have to be propagated directly after flowering; they may also be divided then. Grow in full sun in well-drained poor soil; most pinks also make good rock-garden plants. Petals have culinary and medicinal uses; dried petals are included in scented sachets.

Echinacea purpurea
Echinacea, purple coneflower
Hardy perennial that grows to 1.2 m (4 ft). Sow seed in early spring in a plug tray in greenhouse or propagator, or divide existing plants (in autumn or spring) and plant in border or herb garden. Grow in well-drained soil that will retain a bit of moisture in full sun. Echinacea seems to boost the immune system, thereby helping the body to fight infection, and is used extensively in the pharmaceutical industry. There are several good ornamental cultivars.

Eruca versicaria
Rocket/arugula
Half-hardy annual with a height of 60–90 cm (2–3 ft) in flower. Leaves are oval or lance-shaped; flowers are whitish with darker veining. Sow seed from spring onwards in partial shade in moisture-retentive soil. Sow in autumn for winter salads. Cover with a cloche in severe weather. Hard frost and snow will kill rocket/arugula, but in mild areas it can be harvested for most of the winter. Adds peppery vigour to salads and cold dishes.

Eucalyptus citriodora
Eucalyptus
Tender evergreen tree. Can grow to more than 30 m (100 ft) in its native habitat. A good scented conservatory plant that can be taken outside to a sheltered patio. Sow seed in winter or spring. If kept in pots, feed during growing season. Used in cosmetics and pharmaceuticals.

Foeniculum vulgare
Fennel
Growing to 2.1 m (7 ft) in height, with a spread of 45 cm (18 in), this short-lived perennial is best sown straight into a permanent site. Cultivated for its culinary and medicinal purposes, fennel, especially the bronze form, is also a useful ornamental; its yellow flowers are carried in umbels in summer.

Fragaria vesca
Wild strawberry
Hardy perennial that grows to 15–30 cm (6–12 in). Leaves are divided into heavily serrated leaflets. White-petalled flowers and sweet, scented fruit that may be red or white. Sow seed in late winter or early spring in pots in the greenhouse, or divide existing plants after fruiting. Grow in fertile moist soil in full sun or part shade.

Galium odoratum
syn. *Asperula odorata*
Sweet woodruff
Hardy perennial. Grows to 20 cm (8 in) in flower and has an indefinite spread. Whole plant is aromatic. Leaves are mid-green in whorls. Star-shaped white blooms appear in late spring or early summer. A plant for deep shade. Sow seed or propagate from root cuttings at almost any time, but the best time is after flowering; cut back and take small pieces of root to plant in pots or cuttings bed in part shade; water after planting. It will soon reshoot. Grows best in alkaline soil under deciduous shrubs and trees. Woodruff jelly is a delicacy in some parts of Europe.

Helichrysum italicum
Curry plant
Hardy evergreen perennial that grows to 60 cm (24 in) with a spread of up to 1 m (3 ft). Leaves are narrow and silver-felted; yellow button flowers appear in summer. The whole plant has a strong curry scent. Not much used in the kitchen, rather as an ornamental in gardens. Increase by cuttings in spring or autumn. Plant in well-drained soil in full sun. Prolonged wet and cold can kill the plant, so, where winters are severe, grow in a large container or overwinter in a cold greenhouse.

Humulus lupulus
Hops
Hardy perennial herbaceous climber. Grows to 6 m (20 ft). Has male and female flowers on separate plants. Young leaves are heart-shaped; older leaves have three to five lobes. Whole plant is covered with tiny hooks. Sow in autumn in pots and overwinter in a cold frame. Take cuttings or divide female plants in spring or early summer. The golden form of hop is a showy ornamental and can be used in the same way as green hops.

Hyssopus officinalis
Hyssop

Hardy semi-evergreen perennial that grows to 80 cm (32 in) in flower. Leaves are narrow and aromatic; flowers are blue, pink or white depending on variety. 'Rock hyssop', is a good rock-garden or pot plant with dark-blue flowers. Grow in well-drained average soil in full sun. In pots it may need a feed boost if grown in the same soil for several years. Sow seed in plug trays in heated propagator in spring. Cuttings can be taken in late spring and early summer from non-flowering shoots. Seed can also be sown straight into the ground. Thin out if grown as a hedge. Culinary and medicinal plant; use medicinally only on expert advice.

Juniperus communis
Juniper

Slow-growing hardy evergreen shrub or tree that grows to 4 m (25 ft). Needle-like narrow leaves with sharp-pointed tips. Whole plant is aromatic. Sow seed in autumn in pots and overwinter in cold frame or cold greenhouse. Take cuttings in spring or autumn. Do not use juniper berries in pregnancy or if you suffer from kidney problems.

Laurus nobilis
Bay

Tree or small shrub that grows to 8 m (26 ft), with a spread of 3 m (20 ft) or more. Buy as a well-grown ornamental and use surplus leaves for *bouquet garni* or to flavour oil or vinegar. Pick leaves straight from tree or keep a few dried in a jar.

Lavandula species
Lavender

Hardy or half-hardy evergreen perennials. Vary in height, according to species or cultivar, from 30 cm (12 in) to 90 cm (36 in). All species like an open sunny position in fertile well-drained soil. Seed can be sown in autumn or spring in propagator; overwinter autumn-sown seed in cold greenhouse. Seed, except that from *L. stoechas*, is variable. Cut back plants after flowering, for a neat bush trim again in spring. Flower spikes are usually mauve/purple, pale blue or dark blue. Culinary and medicinal herb also used in distilled form in cosmetics.

Levisticum officinale
Lovage

Hardy perennial. Grows to 2 m (6½ ft) with a spread of up to 1 m (3 ft) or more. Grow in rich, moist, well-drained soil in full sun or part shade; sow seed in autumn outside, or in spring in pots in a propagator. Use young leaves in soups and salads; the flavour is better before flowering. Do not take during pregnancy or if you have kidney problems.

Lonicera species
Honeysuckle

L. periclymenum is a deciduous perennial that grows up to 7 m (23 ft). Its fragrant flowers with a pink/red blush are followed by (poisonous) red berries. *L. japonica* is a semi-evergreen deciduous perennial with a height of up to 10 m (30 ft); pale cream flowers turn yellow with age and are followed by black berries (also poisonous). Sow seed in autumn in pots to overwinter outside or in cold frame. Take cuttings in summer or layer at any time. Will grow in sun or part shade in most soils.

Malva sylvestris
Mallow

Biennial or short-lived perennial that, depending on variety, grows to 1.5 m (5 ft). Rounded leaves on basal rosette resemble those of *Alchemilla mollis*, and those that grow up the stem are finely cut or ivy-shaped. Mallows will tolerate most soils, but in overly moist may need staking. Fertile soil in sun or part shade will suit the plants best. Sow seed in autumn and overwinter in cold frame, or sow in spring in cool greenhouse. Seed can also be sown in the garden where the plants are to flower. Used in cooking.

Melissa officinalis
Lemon balm

Hardy perennial that grows to 80 cm (32 in). The golden form, 'All Gold', may need some protection in winter, so mulch with bracken or other foliage and keep this in place with a cloche. Keep 'All Gold' out of full sun or it will scorch. Golden and variegated forms are fine ornamentals; all are good bee plants. Increase by cuttings or division in autumn or spring. Loses its lemon fragrance when cooked, so use fresh in the kitchen.

Mentha
Mint

Grows to various heights depending on species; some are prostrate. Mint has spreading root runners and can be very invasive. The leaves of different species have different aromatic qualities. Most mints grow best in part or full shade and need to be restrained to prevent them from taking over whole beds. Cut back in midsummer to rejuvenate plants. Culinary and medicinal herb. Mint oil may cause an allergic reaction and must not be used on babies.

Monarda didyma
Bergamot, oswego tea, bee balm

Hardy perennial that, depending on species or cultivar, grows to between 75 cm (30 in) and 90 cm (36 ft), with a spread of 45 cm (18 in). Leaves are elliptical, sometimes toothed, with pointed tips. Flowers are in whorls; colours include pale purple, red, white, soft pink and purple. All cultivars have to be increased by division or cuttings. Seed from species should be sown in propagators. Grow in part shade in moist rich soil; in moisture-retentive soil it will grow in full sun. Mostly grown in herbaceous borders for its flowers, but also has culinary and medicinal uses.

Myrrhis odorata
Sweet Cicely

Hardy perennial that grows to between 60 cm (2 ft) and 90 cm (3 ft) in flower. Leaves are fern-like; small white flowers in large umbels. Sow seed in pots and overwinter in a cold frame because seeds need stratifying. Root cuttings can be taken in spring or autumn, and plants can be divided in spring. For best results, grow in well-drained poor soil. Cut back flower heads before they set seed.

Myrtus communis
Myrtle

Half-hardy evergreen shrub that grows to 3 m (10 ft). All parts are aromatic. In areas with cold wet winters and prolonged ground and air frosts, grow in pots and overwinter in frost-free greenhouse or conservatory. In milder areas, simply protect from too much winter rain. Grow in well-drained soil in full sun. If grown in pots, add grit and

Hyssopus officinalis Hyssop

Monarda didyma Bergamot

Oenothera biennis Evening primrose

bark to loam-based compost. Take soft wood cuttings in spring and semi-ripe cuttings in late summer.

Ocimum basilicum
Basil
In temperate northern Europe basil is usually pot-grown, reaching 45 cm (18 in) with a spread of up to 30 cm (12 in). In Mediterranean regions it grows to twice the size or more, in the ground. Sow seed in spring either direct into the ground after frost, or into containers placed in a warm greenhouse or propagator. Transplant to a larger area as soon as the plant is big enough to handle. Take care not to overwater. Wonderful in salads, in pesto sauce and with pasta.

Oenothera biennis
Evening primrose
Hardy biennial that can reach 1.2 m (4 ft). Lance-shaped leaves make a rosette in the first year, and in the second year the flower spike rises with large yellow, evening-scented flowers. Sow seed in spring in plug trays or in the place where you want it to grow. Grow in well-drained soil in a sunny position. Self-sows abundantly. Mainly medicinal, but all parts are edible and can be steamed and eaten.

Origanum vulgare
Oregano, marjoram
Several species and varieties; most are hardy in light soil and can grow to a height and a spread of up to 60 cm (24 in). Species can be grown in spring in pots in propagator or *in situ*; soil should be free-

draining and alkaline. Do not overwater, will not thrive in waterlogged soils. Best in full sun. Cultivars will not come true from seed and cuttings should be taken in late spring; plants can also be divided in spring. Used extensively in cooking. An infusion in the bath aids relaxation and a few drops of essential oil on the pillow promotes a good night's sleep.

Papaver somniferum
Opium poppy
Hardy annual. Grows to 90 cm (3 ft). Sow seed in autumn for early flowers and seeds, or in spring for later flowering, straight into the ground in a sunny, fertile, well-drained soil. Thin if necessary. Seeds often used in baking breads, cakes and sprinkling over salads. Other parts used in pharmaceuticals.

Pelargonium species
Scented pelargoniums
Half-hardy evergreen shrubs that, depending on variety and species, grow to varying heights, from 30 cm to 1 m (12–40 in). Some species can be grown from seed but it is easier to grow them from cuttings, and all cultivars must be grown from cuttings. Take cuttings in summer or autumn as plants are being cut back prior to overwintering in a frost-free site. Grow in full sun in well-drained soil if in the ground; dig and pot up, reduce watering in autumn and keep watering to a minimum over winter. Essential oils are used in aromatherapy. The scented leaves are sometimes used to flavour cakes and desserts but should be removed before serving.

Perilla frutescens
Perilla
Tender annual that makes a good ornamental in the flower border. Taller purple form can reach 90 cm (3 ft). Leaves slightly resemble a stinging nettle; can also be confused with the 'ruffles' type of basil. Start off in greenhouse or propagator. Transplant, and plant out once frosts are over. Grow in light well-drained soil in full sun or light shade. In cold areas grow in pots. Can stand cold a little better than basil, but likes similar treatment.

Petroselinum crispum
Parsley
Hardy biennial growing to 30 cm (12 in), and to 60 cm (24 in) in flower. Greenish-white flowers in second year. Various forms with heavily curled foliage; others with uncurled, flat leaves. All are good for salads and flavouring. Seeds are chewed in some countries as a remedy for bad breath. Also has a medicinal use but should be avoided during pregnancy.

Pimpinella anisum
Aniseed
Half-hardy annual. Grows to 45 cm (18 in) with a spread of 25 cm (10 in). Sow seed in light well-drained soil in a sunny position when frosts are over. Do not transplant; thin out to 20 cm (8 in) apart. Gather seeds on stalks in late summer just as they ripen, and dry off in paper bags. Seeds used in fruit dishes and Middle Eastern recipes.

Rosa* 'Moonlight'** Rose   ***Saponaria officinalis Soapwort   ***Tropaeoleum majus*** Nasturtium

Portulaca oleracea
Purslane
Half-hardy annual growing to 15 cm
(6 in) with a spread of 30 cm (12 in).
Green or golden leaves. Sow in plug trays
for early planting out or in rows in full
sun; thin out and use early in season.
Mild-flavoured leaves are good in salads
and complement stronger-flavoured
herbs and spices.

Primula vulgaris
Primrose
Spring-flowering perennial. Height and
spread of 15 cm (6 in). Club-shaped
leaves grow from basal rosette. Pale-
yellow flowers with delicate honey scent
grow singly from the rosette. Grows in
moist soil in sun or shade and tolerates
heavy soils. Start seed off in pots in
autumn. Leave outside in cold frame or
grow fresh seed straight after harvest;
germination can be erratic. Plants can be
divided in autumn. Culinary and
medicinal uses.

Rosa species
Rose
Old-fashioned roses, especially the
scented apothecary's rose, *R. gallica*
'Officinalis', were traditionally used in
herb gardens. Lax sprawling growth.
Scented petals are used in cosmetics,
to flavour food and in potpourri.

Rosmarinus officinalis
Rosemary
Numerous cultivars, some upright and
others prostrate. Prostrate group reaches
a height of 30 cm (12 in). The largest
rosemary has a height and a spread of up

to 2 m (6 ½ ft). *R. officinalis* can be grown
from seed, but cultivars need to be
propagated from soft or semi-ripe
cuttings in spring or late summer; they
can also be layered. Needs well-drained
soil and a sunny position. Grows well in
containers. Used in the kitchen,
medicinally and in cosmetic preparations,
but avoid during pregnancy. Essential oil
must not be taken internally.

Rumex acetosa
Sorrel
Sorrel and buckler leaf sorrel (*R. scutatus*)
are useful garden plants. Buckler leaf sorrel
grows to 15–45 cm (6–18 in) with a spread
of 12.5–60 cm (5–24 in). French sorrel is a
hardy perennial growing to 60–120 cm
(2–4 ft) with a spread of 30 cm (1 ft). Sow
seed in spring in propagator from February
onwards, or in late spring outside. Can be
divided in spring or autumn. A good
culinary plant; also used in medicine and,
with alum as a mordant, makes a yellow or
green dye. Contains oxalic acid, making it
poisonous in large doses. People with
kidney disease, rheumatism, gout or
kidney stones should avoid.

Salvia officinalis
Sage
Height and spread vary, depending on
species, up to 90 cm (3 ft) in height and
70 cm (28 in) spread. Purple, golden and
tricoloured sages are good ornamentals
as well as culinary and medicinal plants.
Ideal container plant for a sunny patio.
Not all sages are hardy. *S. elegans*
(pineapple-scented leaves) needs to be
overwintered in frost-free conditions.
Grow from cuttings in spring and

summer and replace plants every few
years as they become very woody. Grow
in a light free-draining soil in full sun.
Dried leaves can be added to potpourri.

Sambucus nigra
Elder
Deciduous hardy perennial shrub or tree.
Grows to 3–7 m (10–23 ft) with a spread
of up to 3.5 m (12 ft). Good ornamental
for borders or wild hedgerows. Fruit must
be cooked if used in the kitchen. Flowers
used to make fritters and elderflower
champagne. Traditionally berries have
been made into a cordial for relieving the
symptoms of colds and coughs.

Sanguisorba minor
Salad burnet
Hardy evergreen perennial. Grows to 20–
60 cm (8–24 in) with a spread of 30 cm
(12 in). Sow seed in spring or autumn; be
sure to deadhead regularly. Culinary and
medicinal herb, much under-used in the
kitchen. Has a slight taste of cucumber
and goes well with fish, cheese and
salads, especially in winter, when other
herbs may be scarce.

Saponaria officinalis
Soapwort
Hardy perennial growing to 90 cm (3 ft)
or more. Tumbling lax plant with lance-
shaped oval leaves and clusters of single
flowers, but 'Rubra Plena' has double
flowers that are at first pink and turn red
with age. Can be invasive. Sow seed in
autumn, as soon as ripe, in a cold frame.
Plants appear in spring. Germination is
sometimes erratic. Rootstock can be
divided in autumn or early spring. It has

been used medicinally, in cosmetics and as a traditional ingredient of soap.

Satureja hortensis
Summer savory, bean herb
Half-hardy annual that in flower reaches 30 cm (12 in) with a spread of 20 cm (8 in). Grows bushier if growing tips are harvested often. Sow seed outside when frosts have finished, or sow in plug trays and transplant when soil has warmed up. Whole plant is aromatic. Use leaves before white or mauve flowers appear. Dries well, and is sold dried. Used widely throughout Europe in dishes that incorporate beans.

Satureja montana
Winter savory, mountain savory
Semi-evergreen hardy perennial that grows to 30 cm (12 in) with a spread of 30 cm (12 in) or more depending on conditions. Narrow, lance-shaped leaves; white flowers; very aromatic. Likes full sun and well-drained poor soil. Good ornamental in the right soil; suitable for rockeries. Take cuttings in spring, or sow seed in propagator or greenhouse in early spring. Seed needs light to germinate. In areas of high rainfall and heavy soil, overwinter some plants in pots, where watering can be minimized. Used to flavour soups and meats.

Sesame indicum
Sesame
Annual tropical herb that grows to 60–90 cm (2–3 ft). Needs long hot summers to produce its nutty seeds. Collect seeds as they ripen before the capsules burst open. Sow after frost danger is past. In cool areas grow under cover. Start in pots in heated propagator to extend growing season. Leaves and seeds used in cooking.

Symphytum officinale
Comfrey
Hardy perennial growing to 1 m (3 ft). Lance-shaped bristly leaves; depending on species or cultivar, flowers can be cream, yellow, blue purple, pink or red. Sow seed in spring in garden; germination is erratic. Root cuttings or divisions produce plants more quickly. Grow in full sun or part shade; does best in deep moist soil. Used in organic gardening as liquid manure.

Tanacetum parthenium
Feverfew
Hardy short-lived perennial. Height varies from 60 cm (2 ft) to 120 cm (4 ft); sometimes smaller, especially golden feverfew, T. parthenium 'Aureum', which reaches 45 cm (18 in) in flower. Grow in rich soil in full sun. Deadhead often. Sow seed in spring or early autumn; overwinter plants from autumn sowing in cold frame or heated greenhouse. Used to relieve migraines but side effects can be unpleasant.

Taraxacum officinale
Dandelion
Hardy perennial. Height in flower about 25 cm (10 in). Long, deeply toothed leaves grow from basal rosette; flowers are deep yellow. Sow seed in spring in pots or straight into soil. Root cuttings can also be taken. Leaves are added to salads; before use, cover plants for a few weeks so they are blanched and less bitter.

Thymus vulgaris
Thyme
Numerous species, some upright, others creeping. Creeping thymes reach about 2.5 cm (1 in) with a spread of 20 cm (8 in) or more. Shrubby thymes reach 30 cm (12 in) with a spread of 20 cm (8 in). Creeping thymes are useful as ground cover or for scented lawns in full sun. Seed of species can be sown on top of a gritty compost. Cultivars are increased only by cuttings; creeping thymes can be increased by division. Deadhead after flowering. The plant is safely eaten in a many dishes, but the oil should be used only on medical advice. Avoid during pregnancy.

Tropaeoleum majus
Nasturtium
Half-hardy annual. Many cultivated forms that creep or are bushy, so height and spread can vary. Height is usually 20–30 cm (8–12 in), and spread can be a metre (40 in) or more. T. majus 'Alaska' has variegated leaves and yellow, orange or red flowers. Good plant for a sunny garden and well-drained poor soil. If overfed, flower production suffers. Sow early in containers, or in situ when danger of frost is past. Deadhead regularly. Seeds, fresh flowers and leaves all edible, but treat with caution.

Urtica dioica
Nettle
Hardy perennial. Grows to 1.5 m (5 ft); in good soil the flowering tops can be even taller. Leaves are arrow-shaped and deeply serrated, with bristles that break off when touched. Grows in any soil in sun or shade. Roots can also be divided and replanted. A good plant for attracting butterflies. Used medicinally, in cooking, in organic gardening and as a dye plant.

Verbena officinalis
Vervain
Hardy perennial growing to 60–90 cm (24–36 in) when in flower. Leaves are deeply lobed; flowers pale lilac. Sow seed in spring in pots or straight into soil. Grows in any well-drained soil in full sun. Divide existing plants in spring or autumn. Avoid during pregnancy.

Viola officinalis
Violet
Hardy perennial that can reach 20 cm (8 in), depending on species. Leaves, usually heart-shaped, grow from basal rosette. Scented flowers in a range of colours; dog violet and wood violet have blue or lilac flowers. Sow seed as soon as ripe in autumn and overwinter in a cold frame. Divide or take cuttings from cultivars or a good plant of a species in spring. Grows in moderately heavy fertile soil. Flowers can be used in herbal sachets and perfumes.

Viola tricolor
Heartsease
Hardy perennial that is often grown as an annual. Grows to 30 cm (12 in). Scalloped mid-green leaves; tricoloured pretty 'little face' flowers. Sow seed in spring in cold frame. Grows best in most soils in sun or part shade. Culinary and medicinal herb.

Zingiber officinale
Ginger
Perennial tropical herb. Grown in a container from a division of its rhizome. Needs peat and loam mixture with added grit and sharp sand. Water freely in hot summer months; reduce watering towards winter. Widely used in eastern cuisines.

suppliers

UK
SUPPLIERS OF PLANTS AND SEEDS

Angelica's Herbs
www.angelicasherbs.co.uk

Beans and Herbs
www.beansandherbs.co.uk

Blackbrook Herb Gardens
www.blackbrookherbgardens.co.uk

Bodmin Plant & Herb Nursery
www.bodminnursery.co.uk

Brin Herb Nursery
www.brinherbnursery.co.uk

Candlesby Herbs
www.candlesbyherbs.co.uk

Chiltern Seeds
www.chilternseeds.co.uk

The Cottage Herbery
www.thecottageherbery.co.uk

CN Seeds Ltd
www.cnseeds.co.uk

Dobies of Devon
www.dobies.co.uk

Downderry Nursery
www.downderry-nursery.co.uk

Edulis
www.edulis.co.uk

Franchi Seeds of Italy
www.seedsofitaly.com

Herb Pharm
www.herb-pharm.com

The Herb Farm
www.herbfarm.co.uk

The Herb Garden & Historical
Plant Nursery
www.historicalplants.co.uk

The Herb Nursery
www.herbnursery.co.uk

Herbal Haven
www.herbalhaven.com

Highdown Nursery
www.highdownnursery.com

Hooksgreen Herbs
www.hooksgreenherbs.com

Hurst Brook Plants
www.hurstbrookplants.co.uk

Iden Croft Herbs
www.uk-herbs.com

Jekka's Herb Farm
www.jekkasherbfarm.com

Johnsons Seeds
www.johnsons-seeds.com

Laurel Farm Herbs
www.laurelfarmherbs.co.uk

Mr. Fothergill's Seeds
www.mr-fothergills.co.uk

Norfolk Herbs
www.norfolkherbs.co.uk

Norfolk Lavender
www.norfolk-lavender.co.uk

The Organic Gardening Catalogue
www.gardenorganic.org.uk

Poyntzfield Herb Nursery
www.poyntzfieldherbs.co.uk

Pepperpot Herbs
www.pepperpotherbplants.co.uk

Pennard Plants
www.pennardplants.com

Samarès Manor Gardens
www.samaresmanor.com

Stonecrop Herbs
www.stonecropnurseries.co.uk

Suffolk Herbs (Kings Seeds)
www.kingsseeds.com

Suttons Seeds
www.suttons.co.uk

Thompson & Morgan Seeds
www.thompson-morgan.com

Urban Herbs
www.urban-herbs.co.uk

Yorkshire Lavender
www.yorkshirelavender.com

DRIED HERBS
AND HERBAL PRODUCTS

Baldwin & Co
www.baldwins.co.uk

The Cotswold Perfumery
www.cotswold-perfumery.co.uk

Daisy Gifts Ltd
www.daisyshop.co.uk

Findhorn Flower Essences
www.findhornessences.com

Hambleden Herbs
www.hambledenherbs.com

Napiers the Herbalists
www.napiers.net

Neal's Yard Remedies
www.nealsyardremedies.com

Potters Herbal Supplies
www.pottersherbals.co.uk

Shirley Price Aromatherapy
www.shirleyprice.co.uk

The Spice Shop
www.thespiceshop.co.uk

Verde London
www.verde.co.uk

OTHER USEFUL RESOURCES

The Herb Society
www.herbsociety.org.uk

US AND CANADA
SUPPLIERS OF PLANTS AND SEEDS

Applewood Seed Co.
www.applewoodseed.com

Avant Gardens
www.avantgardensNE.com

The Banana Tree Inc.
www.banana-tree.com

Bluestone Perennials
www.bluestoneperennials.com

W. Atlee Burpee Seed Co.
www.burpee.com

Companion Plants
www.companionplants.com

The Cook's Garden
www.cooksgarden.com

DeBaggio Herbs
www.debaggioherbs.com

Filaree Farm
www.filareefarm.com

Glasshouse Works
www.rareplants.com

Goodwin Creek Gardens
www.goodwincreekgardens.com

Gurney's Seed
www.gurneys.com

Harris Seeds
www.harrisseeds.com

HerbCo International
www.herbco.net

Heronswood
www.heronswood.com

Horizon Herbs
www.horizonherbs.com

Johnny's Selected Seeds
www.johnnyseeds.com

Logee's Greenhouses
www.logees.com

Mellinger's Inc.
www.mellingers.com

Nichols Garden Nursery
www.nicholsgardennursery.com

Park Seed
www.parkseed.com

Peaceful Valley Farm Supply
www.groworganic.com

Redwood City Seed Company
www.redwoodcityseed.com

Richters Herbs
www.richters.com

Sandy Mush Herb Nursery
www.sandymushherbs.com

Seeds of Change
www.seedsofchange.com

Select Seeds
www.selectseeds.com

Stokes
www.stokeseeds.com

Territorial Seed Company
www.territorialseed.com

The Thyme Garden
www.thymegarden.com

Wayside Gardens
www.waysidegardens.com

West Coast Seeds
www.westcoastseeds.com

White Flower Farm
www.whiteflowerfarm.com

DRIED HERBS
AND HERBAL PRODUCTS

Gaia Herbs
www.gaiaherbs.com

Glenbrook Farms
www.glenbrookfarm.com

Herb Affair
www.herbaffair.com

I herb
www.iherb.com

Leaves and Roots
www.leavesandroots.com

Mountain Rose Herbs
www.mountainroseherbs.com

Remedies Herb Shop
www.remediesherbshop.com

San Francisco Herb Co.
www.sfherb.com

Target Stores
www.target.com

OTHER USEFUL RESOURCES

The Herb Society
www.herbsociety.org

index

Page numbers in *italic* refer to the illustrations

credits

Barbara Segall would like to thank Gisela Mirwis for her research and Debbie Arden and Ruth Ridley (daisyshop.co.uk), who helped to compile the list of herb farms, nurseries and seed suppliers.

Rose Hammick would like to thank Carol Hammick and Adam Tindle for the use of the glasshouse and vegetable garden, Claire Farrow and William Morris, Zosia at White and Gray, Victoria Robinson, Amanda and Sarah Vesey, Georgina Hammick, Katie Rudaz, Richard Mole, Charlotte Packer, Clementine Young and Ashley Western.

All photography by Caroline Arber and William Lingwood apart from pages:
1 ph Debi Treloar
2, 3, 6, 8-9, 101 ph Erin Kunkel
41 below ph Jonathan Buckley
86 ph Rachel Whiting; The family home of Rebecca Proctor in Cornwall www.futurusticblog.com
88, 90, 91, 93-98, 100, 103-106, 108, 109, 111, 114 ph Ian Wallace
92 ph Matt Russell
99, 107 ph Peter Cassidy
102, 110 ph Clare Winfield
112, 113 ph William Lingwood
125 ph Heini Schneebeli and Caroline Hughes

Frontcover ph Emma Mitchell
Backcover ph Simon Brown
Spine ph Erin Kunckel

Key: a = above, b = below, l = left, r = right, c = centre

36 a, 37 & 39 Rosemary Titterington at Iden Croft Herbs, Staplehurst, Kent; 40–41 Bruisyard Vineyard & Herb Centre, Bruisyard, Suffolk; 40 b Rosemary Titterington at Iden Croft Herbs, Staplehurst, Kent; 40 a photograph © Jonathan Buckley; 42–43 Merryweather's Herbs in Herstmonceux, East Sussex; 46 Rosemary Titterington at Iden Croft Herbs, Staplehurst, Kent; 47 & 48 Bruisyard Vineyard & Herb Centre, Bruisyard, Suffolk; 49 Rosemary Titterington at Iden Croft Herbs, Staplehurst, Kent; 52–53 Bruisyard Vineyard & Herb Centre, Bruisyard, Suffolk; 56–57 Linda Garman's home in London; 58 a Rosanna Dickinson's home in London; 58 b & 59 Mary MacCarthy's house in Norfolk; 60–61 Rosanna Dickinson's home in London; 64 & 65 l Linda Garman's home in London; 66–67 Linda Garman's home in London; 68 Mary MacCarthy's house in Norfolk; 70 r & 76 b Linda Garman's home in London; 76 a, 77 & 80 l Mary MacCarthy's house in Norfolk; 80 r Linda Garman's home in London; 81 Mary MacCarthy's house in Norfolk; 85 & 128 Rosanna Dickinson's home in London.